Preaching as Poetry

Also by the Author

Broken Words: Reflections on the Craft of Preaching
A Concise History of Preaching
The Four Pages of the Sermon
God Sense: Reading the Bible for Preaching
Imagination of the Heart: New Understandings in Preaching
The Practice of Preaching
Setting Words on Fire: Putting God at the Center of the Sermon

Edited by the Author

Abingdon Theological Companion to the Lectionary, Preaching Year A, B, C

Coedited by the Author

The New Interpreter's Handbook on Preaching

The Artistry of Preaching Series

Preaching as Poetry

Beauty, Goodness, and Truth in Every Sermon

Paul Scott Wilson

Abingdon Press
Nashville

PREACHING AS POETRY:
BEAUTY, GOODNESS, AND TRUTH IN EVERY SERMON

This book is printed on acid-free paper.

Library of Congress Cataloging-in-Publication Data

Wilson, Paul Scott, 1949-
Preaching as poetry : beauty, goodness, and truth in every sermon / Paul Scott Wilson.
pages cm.—(Artistry of preaching series; 1)
ISBN 978-1-4267-6404-2 (pbk. : alk. paper) 1. Preaching. 2. Religious poetry. I. Title.
BV4211.3.W553 2014
251—dc23

2014018917

14 15 16 17 18 19 20 21 22 23—10 9 8 7 6 5 4 3 2 1

MANUFACTURED IN THE UNITED STATES OF AMERICA

Contents

Series Preface

The Artistry of Preaching series gives practical guidance on matters that receive insufficient attention in preaching literature yet are key for preachers who seek greater creative expression in their preaching. Fresh, faithful proclamation requires imagination and creative engagement of the Bible and our world. There is no shortage of commentaries on the Bible and books on biblical interpretation for preaching, but there is a shortage of practical resources to help strengthen the creativity of preachers to facilitate their proclamation of the gospel.

The first volume of this series, *Preaching as Poetry: Beauty, Goodness, and Truth in Every Sermon*, redefines preaching for our current postmodern age. The world has changed. Beauty, goodness, and truth no longer mean what they used to mean as fixed absolute and universal standards. While this may be threatening to some preachers, the new meanings can actually allow preachers fresh and creative ways to proclaim God's love and saving purposes in a rapidly changing world. Preaching needs to be reconceived as a kind of poetry, in the sense of communicating the wondrous beauty of God's saving purposes and promises in troubled times. God needs to be presented in terms of experience and relationships, more than abstractions, and faith needs to be presented as something that adds beauty, goodness, and truth to life. In other words, for a new generation that seeks concrete outcomes and immediate benefits, faith needs to be presented as a relationship with God and neighbor that affords deep meaning and great joy.

The second volume of the series, *Actuality: Real-Life Stories for Sermons That Matter*, by Scott Hoezee, is a resource for preachers who want guidance to be better storytellers or to use story more effectively to communicate with a new generation. There readers will also find a collection of stories that both preach and that can stimulate their imaginations to identify stories from their own contexts. Preachers can easily run out of good stories to use that embody the gospel. The problem is not a shortage of stories; they are all around in everyday events. The task is learning how to harvest them, as will be shown here. Preachers long for good stories, and today's listeners are not content with the canned Internet illustrations that sound artificial and have a predictable moral. Rather they want stories rooted in the actual world in which they live, that depict life as they know it, and that can function as Jesus's stories did, as parables and metaphors that bear God's grace to their hearers.

The aim of the series is to be practical, to provide concrete guidelines and creative exercises for preachers to follow, to assist them in engaging imaginative practice. Preaching is much more than art, yet when we as preachers employ artistry in our preaching, we assist the Holy Spirit in communicating the gospel to a new generation of people seeking God.

Acknowledgments

I am very grateful to The Louisville Institute Sabbatical Grant for Researchers—2013 for an award that made possible extended leave time, and to Victoria University, its Board of Regents, President Paul Gooch and the Principal of Emmanuel College, Mark Toulouse. To my basic degree and graduate students who encourage and inspire me, I am always in debt. Several former students generously donated their time and wisdom to meet with me for a day to talk about my proposal: my thanks to Michael Brooks, Alexa Gilmour, Yohwan Heo, Lorraine Hill, Heather James, Deb McMillan, Mark Schnell, Dale Skinner, Maryann Skinner, and Christine Smaller. Sam Persons Parkes and Moses Kang were members of this group and also supplied valuable research assistance. Eric Rottman, a graduate student at Emory University, and G. Thomas Carter, longtime friend and Instructor of Law at MacEwan University, provided valued feedback. Professor Leonard J. Brooks of the Joseph L. Rotman School of Management at the University of Toronto offered friendship and wise counsel at a crucial point.

I am grateful to my friends and colleagues in the Academy of Homiletics for encouraging conversations. Special thanks are due to Ronald J. Allen for his generous help, especially in an early stage of this project; Robert Reid for instructive conversations and emails; and David Lose for important exchanges concerning his own recent book publication. Stephen Farris, David Jacobsen, Hank Langknecht, John M. Rottman, and Sam Persons Parkes gave valuable feedback to me in various stages of this manuscript. It is stronger for it though they are in no way responsible for its weaknesses.

For the opportunity to develop and share some of these ideas, thanks also are due to the kindness of numerous people responsible for: the Calgary meeting of Worship Matters of the United Church of Canada, the Discipleship Project of the Houston Diocese of the Evangelical Lutheran Church in America, the ACTS DMin in Preaching program at McCormick Seminary in Chicago, the Luther Academy of the Rockies, the DMin in Biblical Preaching program at Luther Seminary, the 2012 fall retreat of the

Diocese of Montreal of the Anglican Church in Canada, the Crucifusion gathering of 2013, the annual Lenten Study Group at Kingsway Lambton United Church, and Yorkminster Park Baptist Church and the Lester Randall Fellowship in Preaching that hosted the Toronto Festival of Preaching, 2013. Thanks to John and Ruth Foster for warm hospitality and friendship in Arlington, Texas, and to countless others who have hosted me in various generous and gracious ways, my deep appreciation for making the time so rich and the task less burdensome.

As always, I am profoundly indebted to my dear wife, Deanna Wilson, who is a steady guide and constant source of love and support, and without whom this project might not have got off the ground.

Introduction

In this age we have a chance to reconceive biblical preaching, not just how to do it but how to do it better, and how to understand better what we do. The Old Homiletics point forms and hierarchical notions of authority and argument have been largely displaced in the last half-century by the New Homiletic, with its horizontal emphasis on conversational narrative and the needs of the listener. Now, as the church increasingly finds itself in a time of crisis and regrouping, a new vision is needed. We have the opportunity to reexamine how preaching might better meet the vertical, horizontal, and multidirectional needs of this changed world. Preaching needs to be artistic, creative, authentic, apologetic, and contextual, to find ways to speak to a culture whose basic values have changed, and to find fresh ways to speak of God.

Postmodernism is the biggest thing to hit Western cultures and the church since what—the printing press? the automobile? television? the Internet? Then why do so few of us really understand it? Ask folks what it is, and you'll typically receive this sort of response: "I don't know. I've heard of it. Never did know what it was. Never will." Yet we see it all around us. For some people it is just a word that means we don't understand something. "It's the way young people are today; they're postmodern." "Who designed that building—is it postmodern?" If someone were to announce that postmodernism is dead, would anyone rush from the room in tears? Even people who have grown up knowing they are postmodern struggle to know fully what that means. Maybe the nature of postmodernism is that we do not understand it, or if we think we do we'd better think again.

Our age goes by many names, postmodern, postsecular, post-Enlightenment, post-Christian, post-theist. We have poststructuralist philosophy and postcolonial theory. No wonder people may be confused when the age is named for what came before it and not what it is. For our purposes, *postmodern* refers to a negative reaction to the Enlightenment and its overemphasis on reason and its overconfidence in defining knowledge. What we now call postmodern probably has been present throughout the modern era as a kind of alter ego, critiquing and dismantling. In other words, the movement from modern to postmodern is not strictly chronological (though it may feel chronological to some people encountering it for the first time) nor is it uniform. Vast nations are still largely modern in their ways of thinking and administration. Yet in Western culture, to many people the surfacing of postmodern consciousness seems sudden, even though aspects of it have been with us in some cases for centuries, without our awareness.

Use of the term *postmodern* began in earnest in the twentieth century in the arts. Lately postmodern thinking has increasingly come out of the cultural shadows and its ways now tend to dominate. Goodness is relative, truth is questioned, knowledge is challenged, authority is undermined, and skepticism is rampant. Postmodernism is not an organized movement; it is more a set of attitudes that reveal certain illusions beneath modernist assumptions. These attitudes have become so pervasive in our culture, integrated in our thoughts, feelings, and behaviors. Postmodernism is increasingly our way of *being*. Yet the nineteenth- and twentieth-century mind-set of modernism is still lively and present. And so the two realities exist in dynamic tension, while postmodernism generally waxes and modernism wanes, and every modern institution is feeling the pressures of change.

This is a book about how to be more imaginative in preaching. In fact, it is the first of a series devoted to artistry in preaching. This volume reflects the outcome of personal wrestling with many postmodern attitudes, the changing role of the preacher, the seeming relative nature of morality and ethics, the function of a sermon if truth is denied. I take an open attitude toward many of the cultural changes, and I write to encourage several groups of people: (1) Preachers who want to be creative while speaking to the changed needs of the world around them. (2) Preachers who are uncertain how to respond to changing attitudes toward ministry and the church. Some preachers feel a sense of disorientation and vocational questioning. The ministry that they thought they were called to has changed, and many feel less confident and less creative. (3) Preachers who consider themselves postmodern and struggle to understand lingering modern resistance in the church. (4) Students trying to discern their role as preachers today and how best to preach. Many lack clarity about their future roles since modernist theological arguments may seem less satisfying than they once were. (5) Lay people who value preaching and seek guidance in relation to friends and family who are ambivalent toward the church.

> This is a book about how to be more imaginative in preaching.

One thing is clear, we are in the midst of an enormous paradigm shift in Western cultures. Both modernists and postmodernists need to learn the meanings of those terms. Even those modernists who have familiarity with postmodernism may not appreciate the degree to which modernist attitudes and uses of language may hinder effective communication to new generations. Whether postmodern philosophy lives or dies, its effects will be with us for generations to come. Many words remain the same, but their meaning has changed. Unity was once good, now it can be oppressive; history was once valued, now it is questioned; knowledge was once obvious, now it is challenged; truth was once certain, now it is relative. To readers who think that the changes that are discussed here are small and can be readily accommodated, that is not likely to be the case. The changes called for are much deeper than they may first appear. In some ways we need to die to old ways of viewing things to live for the new, much as Jesus taught concerning the need to be "born from above" (John 3:4 NRSV). If we can be open to the changes, they offer much hope for the future of the church.

Postmodernism departs from modern assumptions and mistrusts all grand theories, ideologies, and standardized notions of what is knowledge and art. What we now call postmodern has been present as a reaction against the modern, probably since the Enlightenment project began. In the last fifty years, however, particularly in the wake of the Vietnam War, birth control, the civil rights movement, and other social forces, postmodern attitudes increasingly have become the norm. For example, where children in modern times were taught to be quiet if they did not like something, now children are taught to learn by inquiry and conversation.

The impact of these changes on society, so many of them for the good, is huge. It is as though a transport trailer has flipped on the curve of the road, its load strewn in the tidy flower garden of modernity, and everything seems affected. It is hard to know what can remain standing. From one perspective it looks like chaos. Ideas that seemed like God created them are now exposed as flawed. This is not the simple pendulum swing that often occurs in behavior between one generation and the next. This is a change so monumental and foundational it affects every person, discipline, and institution, aided and abetted by the rise of social media. The impact is likely to be larger than the Enlightenment itself. Even basic ideas of truth and goodness seem altered. Pontius Pilate used to seem odd asking "What is truth?" but now Pilate is many of the folks we know, perhaps ourselves. New understandings about how language works have pervasive influence. Reason and logic have taken a hit; they are seen as only one expression of knowledge; values and principles are favored over rules and arguments. Out of this seeming chaos new orders are emerging, and it is important that preachers and their congregations be attuned to it.

Many people may feel that postmodernism is a problem. Another perspective, one taken here, is that modernism is the problem. The world has rapidly changed, and to the degree that the church has been locked in modernist ways, it has not been able to reach new people.

A fourfold imperative emerges in this new cultural landscape: first, that preachers immerse themselves in the mind-set of today in order to be able to speak creatively to a changed world; second, that preachers can benefit from new understandings about how language works—language has new meanings and functions in postmodern culture and some things that used to make sense and be accepted do not make sense to many people any more; third, that the Bible can help preachers recover the poetry of faith; and finally, that preaching will be strengthened by centering on God. This imperative reveals the need for theopoetic preaching, preaching that speaks of God in poetic ways. This is not preaching poems; it is poetic preaching that treasures language—with all of its frail images, symbols, and metaphors—to communicate God. This sort of preaching acknowledges the fragile but powerful beauty of language, which is a critical aspect of the postmodern life. More than we might be aware, the poetic has been a part of our lives throughout the ages. Paul recognized the frail nature of language when he said "we have this treasure in earthen vessels" (2 Cor 4:7 KJV).

Theopoetic preaching, as envisioned here, is invitational and open to diverse perspectives. It relies on theology yet minimizes abstract speech about God. It uses the language of the Bible in poetic ways and speaks of God acting. It is humble before the mystery of God, and—to be bold in adapting the words of Paul—theopoetry is patient, it is kind, it isn't jealous, it doesn't brag, it isn't arrogant, it isn't rude... it isn't happy with injustice, but it is happy with the truth (see 1 Cor 13:4-6). It sings of the beauty, goodness, and truth of God in fresh ways for a changed world. The following pages present one vision of what theopoetic preaching might be.

Beauty, goodness, and truth are three classical values I use to discuss preaching instead of traditional theological categories, though the latter informs my thinking. These three values are especially appropriate for theopoetry and they need to be in every sermon. Is there anything more beautiful than God and God's purposes? Yet the church has tended to turn faith into much of a chore, perhaps an extension of the Protestant work ethic. Beauty names what preachers offer to the world, the beauty of God, hence a more beautiful life in knowing God and loving our neighbor. Goodness and truth are also beautiful. Goodness is important because preachers struggle with how to preach goodness in a relativistic age when *good* and *bad* are less clear and universally defined than in the modern age. If preachers can appreciate new attitudes toward goodness, that is, if preachers can get into the mindset of many people today, their sermons can offer direction in life and can be received as such. Truth is important because, although the very existence of truth is denied in much postmodern thought, this denial can open the way for preachers more authentically to focus on God. Preachers who attend to these three values may gain confidence and joy in their vocation and may lead people to deeper faith and commitment.

Much scripture is cited throughout these pages. I do this not to proof text, that practice of trying to prove a point by quoting God's Word. I do it rather in order to hold up the Bible as the book whereby Christians live; model the kind of intertextual reading that is helpful in this postmodern age; and embrace the words of the Bible as among the most beautiful that we have. Faith is our finest poetry, and our finest poetry is lived faith.

My own theological perspective need not be the reader's. In the modern period, from which we emerge, people felt it necessary either to reject supernatural elements in the Bible on the basis of reason and science, or to affirm them on the basis of revelation and experience. I am not enamored of the religion or science debate: The either/or choice seems false and creates division. Science and religion need not be mutually exclusive worldviews. Theopoetry takes seriously the biblical language and, to my mind, preachers using it may appeal to people who hear and understand in diverse ways. The nature of language speaks against a tight hold on settled reality that seemed necessary in the age since the Enlightenment. Theopoetry is thus sympathetic to many recent projects, like Eugene Peterson's *Tell It Slant*,[1] Kevin J. Vanhoozer's *Remythologizing Theology*,[2] and others.

A word about structure: The current volume has three sections devoted to beauty, goodness, and truth. Each section has three chapters: the first teaches some aspects of contemporary thought and culture presented as theory; the second connects with homiletics—homiletical theology and theory; and the third "practices what is preached." The three practice chapters demonstrate theopoetic speech without being sermons in themselves. They also highlight key parts of the Christian story—Christmas, Easter, and Pentecost—that I suggest need more frequent reference in preaching because they are so central in forming Christian identity. These chapters loosely focus on the Trinity: God coming in Jesus Christ; Christ exchanging our death for his innocence; and the Holy Spirit descending on the church. These practice chapters further encourage imagination for prophetic and poetic speech.

Part I

Beauty and Unity

Chapter One

Preaching as Poetry in an Age of Math (Theory)

The problem facing the church in the twenty-first century is not postmodernism, it is modernism. Postmodernity is a not a problem for most of the young; it is their way of thought. It is a problem for those who have inherited modernist assumptions. Moreover, we all have modernity and postmodernity in us because they are in our culture and blood. These tumultuous times have so much in flux that preachers may need a fresh vision of what they are doing. Moreover, people in the culture may need a fresh vision of what the church has to offer them. The church could try to imitate what it finds around it in society, for instance, in the entertainment world or the business community, and thus try to make its message more appealing. The alternate suggestion here is that preachers name what is distinctive about the church and focus their efforts there. What the church offers by way of appreciative critique and what the culture offers are as different as poetry is to math. My hope is that preachers may be inspired to think of themselves as offering a kind of poetry to the world and thereby gain fresh confidence and hope for their tasks. They are pastors to be sure, but they are also God's poets-in-residence.

Poetry and Math

Poetry and math are two ways of knowing. There is poetry in math, for instance, in elegant solutions to problems, and there is math in poetry, for instance, in rhythm, rhyme schemes, and word patterns. That said, poetry and math tend to be contrasting ways to think. Math (at least basic math) generalizes from a vast number of particular situations to establish its rules, axioms, theories, and definitions. It is precise and looks for the simplest explanations. In first grade we were taught 1 + 1 = 2, and we were shown numerically representative pictures of apples, kittens, children, mittens, any objects really, and over and over the conclusion of math was the same, 1 + 1 = 2. Math is a way of thinking using logic that is largely indebted to the Enlightenment. Math has many applications to different parts of life. It is the basis for search engines like Google and many sciences upon which economic productivity depends. Math at its basic levels, as arithmetic and for instance math as Isaac Newton taught it, mostly deals with the material world and physical properties. It is rooted in reason and formulas. It is unchanging: more than 2,000 years ago, Pythagoras came up with $a^2 + b^2 = c^2$. In a right-angled triangle, the sum of the squares of the shorter sides equals the length of the hypotenuse squared. In 20,000 years that will still be true. As one scholar notes, in math it seems like truths do exist "out there" as objective, necessary, and unchanging realities: "Many mathematicians, when pressed, admit to being Platonists. The great logician Kurt Gödel argued that mathematical concepts and ideas 'form an objective reality of their own, which we cannot create or change, but only perceive and describe.' "[1] Math is an efficient way to communicate, reducing things to their basics, relying more on numbers than words. At least until the collapse of Newtonian math and logic, math abhored contradiction and paradox.[2]

Math is a good metaphor for popular ways of thinking: Some young people in my own family speak at a faster rate than data travels on the Internet. Whole sentences are one long varied but uninterrupted sound with a slight rise at the end as though asking a question followed by a split second for breath. Clearly even youth are feeling the pressure: People want short answers, general truths, precise, simple responses, and quick exchanges of information in short bursts of twittered conversation. People want to be finished with one thing and on to the next connection and Internet link. Long answers, theory, and reviews of history provoke impatience.

A problem arises for the church in this age because much of the Christian faith is poetry. There is math in how some of the creeds are understood or moral rules are applied, but generally the way of thinking that faith calls for is poetry. It probes the depths of pain and brokenness within and around us, it points to the stunning beauty of God's love, and it opens us to mystery. In contrast to math, poetry looks more at particular than general events, and concentrates on what makes things unique. Poetry often needs interpretation; it may not fully communicate instantly. It invites relationship and beckons us to stay awhile rather than rushing off. It may raise more questions than it answers. It relies on words, not numbers, and often deliberately highlights contradictions and paradox. It does not seek to solve problems so much as to describe situations. Robert Frost's "The Road Not Taken," will not tell anyone facing a decision what to do, it simply tells the reader what Frost did (he took the road "less traveled by"). But it also creates for the reader Frost's autumn experience, which in itself may unlock memories, feelings, and possible direction. Poetry deals with emotional, material, and spiritual matters all together. It is precise in many ways, but it also invites multiple meanings. Poetry takes time to savor and appreciate. It is associated with creativity and imagination, with things not practical. Thus some people discard poetry.

Why Math May Not Work

The temptation of the church in this age may be to adjust its message for the practical math mind-set. Preachers in this age have already done this with the wide adoption of PowerPoint to project outlines of sermons. They have adjusted, leaned into math, by underscoring and organizing their sermons with graphics, as in academic-type lectures. Some preachers may be encouraged to talk faster, as much of the culture does, so the sermon does not take so long. Or, they may offer summary statements of church teachings, or hand out fill-in-the-blank sermon outline forms, or post sermon themes on Twitter accounts, compact bursts of important information, or give renewed emphasis to propositional and cognate learning. This might seem nicely to conform to the ways of math. Some of these changes may be important. However, math may not work for several reasons:

(1) Christianity is unlikely to appeal to a postmodern mind-set that is suspicious of organized religion and closed systems of predetermined truths. People tend not to be interested in joining something to which they can bring little, where the problems have already been resolved and the answers determined.

(2) The church in some ways is at a disadvantage in being necessarily rooted in history, a subject for which there is relatively little patience. During the Enlightenment, the growth of history as a discipline provided new ways of looking at the world. History was important. Most knowledge lay in the past and needed recovery. The mantra went: Learn from history so as not to repeat the mistakes of the past in the future. If past, present, and future were a teeter-totter, in the modern era it would tilt down toward history, such was its weight and importance. Now, in a postmodern era, the

teeter-totter tilts down toward the future. People say "that's history" as a way to dismiss something. They do not generally care about where things came from so much as where things are going. What is the newest technology, undiscovered business opportunity, or upcoming event? The future is in and the past is out. Young people are typically anxious about their futures. The past seems to have little to teach us, or to offer by way of practical outcome; what counts is information that is expanding exponentially with the help of computers. It comes to us out of the future.

(3) Math is not faith's strength, poetry is. Math and poetry are not necessarily in conflict, but the church in worship should concentrate on its strength. Granted, the world may not be any more patient with poetry than it is with history. Poetry often demands time for processing. Nonetheless, the world today is powerfully attracted by its own versions of some classical values, namely beauty, goodness, and truth. They connect with poetry. In the presence of beauty, goodness, and truth, most people I know want more, not less, and they do not mind spending time. All three values have undergone a postmodern change. If the church can learn from these changes, and build on the broad appeal that they have, its poetry may find reception.

(4) The language of spirituality is not certainty but poetry. As Hebrews puts it, "Now faith is the assurance of things hoped for, the conviction of things not seen." (11:1 NRSV). The contemporary world has a hunger for spirituality. Christian spirituality, as I understand, it is an awareness of God in the ordinary things of life, a sense of who one is in relationship to the world, and an alertness to the possibility of God both in one's neighbor and in ordinary and extraordinary events alike. It offers a sense of meaning both in and beyond oneself. Reason and its formulations are inadequate on their own to portray the sublime that the imagination and poetry are able to represent. Overreliance on reason was a basic failing of the Enlightenment project. Preaching recently has moved away from heavy reliance on propositions and in the direction of story, and now it needs to be reconceived as a kind of poetry.

The Preacher as Poet

Preaching is not poetry in the usual sense. In some limited ways the preacher is like a traditional poet, at least in being sensitive to language, to its limitations, for instance, in capturing the brilliance of a cardinal on a snowy cedar bough. In general, we speak here not of poetry as high art, or of preachers composing sermons in verse with rhyme scheme and meter, as some hip hop artists might be able to do with effect. To exaggerate, the contrast is between preaching as information and preaching as experience, but both are needed. Poetry is a way of pointing to God in the world, of praising God's beauty and love, and finding both mystery and ongoing purpose and meaning, often in the midst of suffering. Poetry here refers to the capacity of the sermon to "put a frame around the mystery," as Frederick Buechner once described preaching, or to awaken a sense of wonder, as Thomas Troegger says.[3] Poetry refers to the sermon's ability to take the fragmented nature of daily life and offer in and through it glimpses of a coherent and meaningful whole and, even more, the hand of a loving God.

Poetry is a way of pointing to God in the world.

The poetry in question is not the preacher's creation but God's, God's purposes seen in and through the events of daily life. The beauty and elegance of the sciences are God-given and included in this poetry, but we are not confined there. The sermon opens windows to show the new creation amidst the old, Christ drawing all things to himself. I like to think that the best words in a sermon come not from the preacher alone, but from the Spirit. Thus each faithful sermon in part is a miracle. That is why, in an ascription of glory that sometimes follows a sermon, preachers say "All thanks be to God," not "All thanks be to me." God's poetry synthesizes, harmonizes, integrates, pulls together; its language portrays divinity infusing the common, ordinary events of each day. In short, preaching can be a source of beauty.

For the ancient Greeks, beauty was a fixed quality. It had to do with pleasing symmetry, proportion, unity, harmony, and balance in art. Aristotle simply said that "the beautiful is what is pleasant to the eyes or to the ears,"[4] and he connected beauty with desire.[5] Together with goodness, he tied it to the origin of all knowledge: What we want motivates us to discover and learn.[6] For purposes of preaching, beauty is the experience of God and God's purposes, the in-breaking of the future now. Jesus called it the realm or kingdom of God. Beauty is discovery of profound meaning beyond oneself, often in seeming contrast to the events of the day. Beauty is fruits of the Spirit: mercy, love, reconciliation, hope, healing, food for the hungry, jobs for the unemployed, peace for the war-torn, hope for the desperate, consolation for the inconsolable, joy for the sorrowful. I use the term *unity* to characterize beauty, because in God one may sense a wondrous unity and coherence beyond what one can fully apprehend and beyond the seeming chaos we may find in events around us. This is not the unity of a closed rational system of thought that seemingly allows no difference or entry—the kind of unity much postmodern thought reacts against. Rather the unity of which we speak is the unity of One who sees humanity in all its variations and contradictions and loves us all equally.

The notion of poetry might seem hopelessly romantic. Beauty may seem like a frill. What about all of the horrible things that happen in the world? They are decidedly not poetry and the sermon must unflinchingly name the worst the world has to offer. Without being voyeuristic or going into detailed horrifying description, it briefly opens portals on life in all of its ugliness, stink, brokenness, horror, sorrow, and sin. The sermon is poetry to the extent that it can do this yet still hold out strong evidence of God's love and saving purposes.

Poetry is not an ingredient the preacher adds to a description of reality; the poetry is to be found in reality when God's reconciling and renewing purposes are considered in the large picture with 360-degree focus. Sorrow, injustice, and lament still speak with their convincing logic, but they do not have the final word. God in Christ has entered the worst, thus poetry may be sought. The poetry of the end times is already heard as music in the present. Its refrains crack the foundations of all the powers that seem to reign. The new reality that this poetry communicates is already breaking in. The reign that will finally rule has already begun. This poetry does not answer all questions nor does it try. As Leonard Cohen sings in his "Anthem," we should forget perfection, because light gets in through the cracks in life. Theopoetry is sacramental; it bears God and all the hope that is needed in this broken world. Paul claims that "no one can say, 'Jesus is Lord,' except by the Holy Spirit" (1 Cor 12:3) and if he is right, only by the Spirit can one write or hear such poetry.

Poetry has the potential to portray a relationship with God as more than good behaving and right thinking. As preachers we may inadvertently have packaged the faith as work to be done, propositions to be unpacked, concepts to be understood, beliefs to be affirmed, formulas to be worked out. We tend to speak as though truth and meaning exist out there like ideas that we only need to grasp and affirm in order for us to be righteous. We may have communicated faith as a thing one has or not, an object one uses to get around in life, like a bike or a car. In daily life, intensity of personal and communal faith varies, questions arise, doubt lingers. Yet for many, the beauty of God, the trust in God's goodness, and the wonder of an ongoing relationship with a saving God abide. To communicate this, we speak of God as a person and of truth as relational. If I portray the kindness of someone at work, I do not go into philosophy; instead I recite the things that happened. Similarly, if I describe my relationship with God, I do not use math or science formulas. As with poetry in general, I use concrete language and focus on specific sensory details to carry meaning. Poetry helps speak of a wonderful relationship. Ideally, through the sermon God in Christ is perceived as a steady and constant friend, and the gospel is experienced as if for the first time.

The preacher is a poet in the sense of being an agent of God's poetry, someone who perceives God's beauty, goodness, and truth. In our own lives, beauty, goodness, and truth come from God. They are treasures God gives. These are given in the sermon, "not as the world gives" (as Jesus said of peace in John 14:27): Beauty is not the world's standard, but what is beautiful in God's sight. As some scholars have noted, our notion of beauty needs to include the death of Jesus on the cross. If it does not then it is at odds with the God who finds that ugliness beautiful. Goodness is God's character. It is what is virtuous and just in God's realm, what can be tasted now as a foretaste of what is to come. And truth is a living truth known in relationship with God.

Faith itself is poetic, having unity and meaning, beauty and coherence, joy and promise. This is different from modernist ways of presenting faith as a closed rational system of thought that one must accept or reject, everything figured out. Living faith involves movement, exploration, discovery, mystery, dance, and play. A relationship with God is a living source of joy, something greatly to be valued like Jesus described: "The kingdom of heaven is like a treasure that somebody hid in a field, which someone else found and covered up. Full of joy, the finder sold everything and bought that field" (Matt 13:44). Were we to speak of faith joyfully, like Jesus did, perhaps more people would joyously seek faith.

Poetry Already

In recent decades preaching has been less frequently conceived as making an intellectual argument or building ideas with abstract points. Preachers seem to be paying more attention to the Bible and to what the listeners need. How successful these approaches have been in terms of holding church members or attracting new ones is a complex matter. Churches are in decline for many reasons. The encouragement here is that we speak with fewer abstractions about God and speak instead in more experiential terms. The focus is less on trying to provide formulas than inviting people to experience God for themselves in and through the Holy Spirit. How might we do that?

Some of what we mean by *poetry* was already present in the modern as a kind of reverse image or underside, but it really came to the fore in the New Homiletic, which had its beginnings in the 1950s:

(1) Words do not have a one-to-one correspondence with reality. Meaning is not straightforward; it requires interpretation and is socially conditioned. In the early 1800s, imagination was regarded as wild and suspect, but poet S. T. Coleridge, in contrast, argued that it opened doors to reality and truth. He elevated imagination above linear ways of thinking, and as a principle tool of poets and theologians. Revaluing imagination for preaching has been a big part of the New Homiletic with its emphasis on image, metaphor, story, and idea.

(2) Poetry recognizes that language, unlike basic math, has many meanings. Horace Bushnell knew this in the 1850s when he argued that biblical texts have many meanings, "even as a stalk of corn pushes out leaf from within leaf by a growth that is its unsheathing."[7] Language functions to communicate many things beyond information and, in metaphor and narrative, can generate experience. We enter biblical texts to experience their meanings; they cannot be reduced to abstract propositions and doctrines, that is, teachings of the church.

(3) Predetermined forms and unexamined assumptions are suspect. The New Homiletic challenged classic modes of point-form preaching by claiming that a sermon should have its own forms, design, functions, and ways of being. Sermons should be organic as opposed to mechanical, as H. Grady Davis was among the first to argue in 1958; they should be "an idea that grows."[8]

(4) "Context is everything" is a frequent mantra of postmodern thought. Already in 1969, David Randolph said of the sermon: "[It] does not arise from religion in general and address the universe.... [It brings] the meaning of the text to expression in the situation of the hearers, rather than by abstraction."[9] Preaching is concrete speech about specific situations as opposed to broad generalizations and intellectual abstractions.

(5) Logic and reason are not the only kinds of learning and knowing. Fred Craddock proposed inductive sermons as opposed to deductive, in his *As One without Authority*[10] in 1971. Charles L. Rice, Eugene Lowry, and a host of others speak in a related manner of sermons proceeding by narrative

plot, in other words, drawing listeners into unfolding action. Sermons proceed in dynamic ways that do not necessarily conform to rational argument.

(6) Story has become a primary vehicle of preaching. Postmodern thought reacts against universal truth claims demanding conformity and suppressing difference. Stories of contemporary people in their contexts are tools to highlight those who have been silenced or oppressed. Narrative is a genre whereby the particular and specific are valued, along with diversity and pluralism. Differences matter.

(7) Words are events. Meaning is fluid and unstable, needing to be renegotiated in each moment. Interpretation is inescapable. These notions correspond well with the sermon as a Word event, a notion derived from the New Hermeneutic in the 1960s. The New Homiletic, inspired by the New Hermeneutic, focused on the eventful nature of metaphor, story, and parable, but here it may have stumbled. The Word event over time seemed to become a word event. At the New Homiletic's worst, stories and the experience they provided seemed to be the point. There was never agreement on the need for God to be the focus of sermons.

Theopoetics

Preaching as poetry is not in the first instance a genre of writing, but is rather a way of seeing. It uses the gospel as its lens. It is not a way of explaining or arguing or defending the faith, but of pointing to the mystery and possibility of an integrated life in God's care. Math emphasizes belief and getting the wrinkles sorted out. Poetry emphasizes faith, taking a risk. M. Craig Barnes has written *The Pastor as Minor Poet* in which he describes the difference between engineers and poets. Some people contribute to society by "following a particular text" and some peer beneath the surface:

> Engineers, for example, follow their textbooks in constructing a bridge that leads across the deep ravines. And one hopes that they have been very, very devoted to those texts. By contrast, a poet who crosses the engineer's bridge will go home and spend all day constructing verse that reveals the longing of the soul to find such an overpass where we stand on the banks of a disaster and peer down into the valley of death.[11]

Such poetry has the ability to embrace contradictions rather than explain them away; it allows for and enhances a sense of mystery even as it points to truths that can be known in ways not limited to strict logic.

Poetry has the ability to embrace contradictions rather than explain them away.

Numerous writers speak at length about how important it is for preachers to have imagination or creativity. For some this artistry is a rhetorical strategy for effective communication—images, metaphors, and stories generate interest. For others, imagination is essential if one wants to communicate God. Gaston Bachelard speaks of "a poetic register that corresponds to the soul."[12] James K. A. Smith sees imagination as being "on a register that flies below the radar of conscious reflection," that produces a unifying world view. He says "the formation of the imagination is a liturgical effect,"[13] by participating in worship over time we develop an awareness of the world that shapes our perception. Preachers must be able to look beyond the limitations of this moment and circumstance to perceive God where God seems not to be. Far from being an exercise in fantasy, it is a way of probing deeper into daily reality. I favor the theological function of imagination while upholding the rhetorical. Imagination allows the preacher to perceive God's beauty and is fully evident throughout the Bible.

Numerous scholars today engage an interdisciplinary area loosely known as theopoetics (combining the root words for God and poetry), first founded by Joseph Campbell, Stanley Romaine Hopper, Amos Wilder, and Paul Tillich, among others. Wilder, whose playwright brother Thornton Wilder wrote *Our Town*, popularized the term *theopoetic* in his book *Theopoetic: Theology and the Religious Imagination* (1976). Theopoetics is an attempt at "the renewal of Christianity… [through] the renewal of its language."[14] "Religious communication," he said, "generally must overcome a long addiction to the discursive, the rationalistic, and the prosaic." He called for more attention to imagination in theology,

> doing more justice to the role of the symbolic and the prerational in the way we deal with experience.… Imagination is a necessary component of all profound knowing and celebration; all remembering, realizing, and anticipating; all faith, hope, and love. When imagination fails doctrines become ossified, witness and proclamation wooden, doxologies and litanies empty, consolations hollow, and ethics legalistic.[15]

Through greater attention to art, symbols, and images, he hoped to recover for theology, "the spontaneous, the sacred, and the mysterious."[16] He wanted to present a creative alternative to supplement systematic theology and its essential rigorous thinking about faith.

Wilder's point seems to have even greater urgency today. Systematic or constructive theology is controlled and linear. It pursues logical structures for experience that at times claims too much certainty or precision and does not sufficiently allow for beauty or mystery. Moreover, it undervalues thinking in images and thereby distorts the experience and realities it seeks to describe. Philosopher of religion Stanley Hopper said, "theopoetics would seem to be a more appropriate way of thinking about the ineffable. Theology tends to develop talk about God logically, where the logos is constrained within the model of Aristotelian propositional thinking; whereas theopoetics stresses the poem dimension, the creativity of God. . . . When we start talking theologically, we lose the poetic."[17] Hopper was bold and more dismissive of dogma and theology than preachers ought to be, for we need all the tools we can get. Still, he makes a good point about the experiential nature of poetic language: "For the model for a theology of the Word is not the model of logic or mathematics, but the model of language—of Logos as primary utterance. . . . Thus a theology founded upon the mathematical models of propositional logic is founded upon a profound metaphysical error: Christ . . . is again fixated to his Cross, and the Kingdom does not come."[18]

Theopoetics is concerned with going beyond the limits of rational discourse and conceptual ways of knowing. Theopoetics contrasts theo-logic, the systematic, rationalistic, discursive discourse that we find in much academic theology, even in some of our own sermons. Even here, in writing about theopoetics I necessarily use a discursive genre to explain it (in the third chapter of each section I switch to greater use of theopoetry). Propositions used sparingly in sermons can be an essential vehicle for the poetry of God. Some discursive theology is valuable to understand faith, but just how much? Theo-logic tends to narrow religious experience to a small portion of life, and in so doing misses much primary experience the Bible talks about. Wilder invited Christians to expand religious imagination and be open to spiritual experiences of the sort that inspire visions, hymns, and poems—awakening the soul. As he said, "Before the message, the vision; before the sermon, the hymn; before the prose, the poem."[19]

Over the last few decades much preaching has effectively used narrative, meeting at least some of the needs about which Wilder spoke. Narrative is one way to think in images. Without rejecting prose and propositions, preachers do not need to put as much emphasis on them as has been common in some quarters. But theopoetics is concerned with more than realizing the imagistic potential *(poetential?)* of language—it is not *poetics* but *theopoetics*. Theopoetics is about God. It represents not a way of reasoning about God, but a way of thinking about God that relies heavily on images, symbols, and story. More than using narrative and imagery to greater theological and biblical effect, it accesses the larger picture of life in light of God's works and plan—larger too than when a single text, doctrine, or issue is the focus of a sermon.

L. B. C. Keefe-Perry represents a new generation of poets. He offers a description of theopoetics that can apply to preaching: "Theopoetics is a type of writing, and I would like to offer that it is a way of perceiving as well. The theopoet as wordsmith can so craft because she sees theopoetically, because she is looking for all the ways her experiences are variations on a Divine theme."[20] Theopoetics seems not so much an activity to engage as a way of being and speaking. For Keefe-Perry, "how we articulate our experience can change our experience."[21]

James K. A. Smith speaks of worship in terms similar to theopoetics. He argues that there is a logic of practice, a way of knowing through action, a way of perceiving the world: "I'm pushing back against an 'intellectualist' account of action that assumes that what I *do* is the outcome of what I *think*. . . . Perception is already an evaluation that then primes me to act in certain ways."[22] Worship combines bodily ways of knowing, or kinaesthetics, with an imagination-shaped worldview, or poetics. "We live *into* the stories we've absorbed; we become characters in the drama that has captivated us. Thus, much of our action is action out a kind of script that has unconsciously captured our imaginations."[23] He wants to relativize the intellect and give due credit to the imagination in predisposing us to certain ways of behavior: "Our action emerges from how we imagine the world."[24] "I can make choices to immerse myself in practices that will re-form my unconscious."[25] In short, preaching can serve to imagine the world in ways different from what it appears to be and thereby it can hope to alter not only behavior but the world.

An Invitational Stance

A compelling feature of theopoetics can be its openness; it welcomes and elicits participation and involvement. Scott Holland says of theopoetics that, "Its narratives lead to other narratives, its metaphors encourage new metaphors, its confessions invoke more confessions, and its conversations invite more conversations."[26] This is the kind of approach the church needs in an age of pluralism and diversity if it is to engage others effectively with the gospel. The experiences that people have of God need to be taken seriously as attempts to make sense and meaning of their encounters with something beyond themselves. Keefe-Perry observes, "A novel feature of theopoetic thought is its invitational stance. Rather than attempt to convince detractors of their errors, an empowered theopoetic would gradually draw them into conversation."[27]

The range of scholars who embrace these kinds of understandings is wide and varied. Some are ready to let go of traditional theology, while others, like myself, feel no need to choose between theopoetics and theo-logic, or between the Bible as revelation and the revelatory potential of creation. The preacher as a theopoet encourages listeners to be theopoets, as alert to what can be captured effectively by language as to what cannot. As long as the church places too much emphasis on theo-logic, faith sounds like a finished project, all certain, a house with shut doors and windows. It can sound fixed and rigid, like we have all the answers in the face of the mystery of God, or like we preachers are trying to prove we are smarter that ordinary believers who thus may feel stupid. Discipleship can be impeded. Theopoetics is a tool for witness and confession. It describes experience realistically yet in the light of faith, death unflinchingly yet in the light of glory, and tomorrow seriously yet in the joy of hope.

Challenges for Preachers

Two challenges for preachers emerge: The first is how to foster an even more invitational stance to encourage others in the congregation to speak about their own spiritual experiences—to speak of God. The modern church encouraged people to accept its truths, where the postmodern needs to welcome inquiry, discussion, active pursuit of truth, and individual witness to it. Through this kind of exchange God may come to be more central for people. The church through scripture may give them language with which to speak. The theopoetic testimony they offer is a creative contribution to the church, something that cannot be appreciated when correct teaching is the only focus.

The second challenge is related: to be more faithful as disciples of Christ. Current generations interested in spiritual experience are not captivated by how the church has processed its thought and answered problems in the past. Denominations are not a draw. Tradition and propositional thinking is central to the church's self-understanding and will continue to be, though it may be used with greater sensitivity, possibly in more open and invitational ways. The church must reconceive of itself while being faithful to the biblical witness. This is probably the most important issue facing the church in this century. How does the church quicken its distinctive identity as people of the Bible while it relates to a radically changed culture?

The church needs to change and we need to be a part of that change, making positive contributions, not be mere onlookers or naysayers. Most important for this journey, we need affirmation that we can change without losing Christian identity or betraying our faith. That is part of the purpose here. Literary deconstruction may help because it calls us to rethink our assumptions and articulate them afresh. It helps us see flaws in the thoughts that we assumed were obvious truth. It gives us new ways to think and new ways to conceive of the gospel. The church needs to affirm what is good in the spiritual experiences of others, inside and outside the Christian faith, and be genuinely open to all, encouraging of their journeys, not to stand in judgment over them. At the same time the church needs somehow to reconceive of the Bible as the Word of God in an age where many seem indifferent to it, and to hold up Jesus Christ as the friend and Savior who makes life beautiful, good, and true.

Chapter Two

The Beauty of Faith (Homiletics)

Why should preachers care about beauty? A preacher who graduated from seminary in the 1990s recently lamented, "I am not sure what I am doing anymore. At weddings people think they have hired me to do what they want, at funerals people ask me not to mention God, and on Sundays I wonder if the Word of God seems to matter." Many preachers are confused about their roles these days. The church, along with culture, is in a time of transition—we know from what but not to what. Still, we have a key role to play in what happens, and beauty can be a significant player in how we reconceive of preaching and faith. Preaching hopefully will always be understood as the Word of God, but in these times some supplemental understandings may help, since for many people, "This is the Word of God" can stop conversation. Perhaps our role as preachers is this: In God's name we offer beauty to the world. Every Sunday we have something beautiful to give, and it is handcrafted language offering meaning and purpose. Here, amidst all the fragments of life today, we offer the One who is Unity itself. That is beautiful. To think of preaching as beautiful can change how we do it and how we feel about our roles.

Classical Beauty

What is beauty? Beauty used to be an external reality that exists "out there." In the so-called great theory of beauty going back to Aristotle, beauty is what pleases by its symmetries, proportions, balance, order, unity, and harmony.[1] Augustine and others found that beauty originates in the mind and character of the divine, and is imparted to creation through the Spirit who in Christ makes all things new.

There was every reason to think that beauty did exist "out there" in the Middle Ages when people found beauty, harmony, and unity everywhere, all pointing to Christ at work "draw[ing] all things to himself"[2] (var., John 12:32), as Duns Scotus Erigena said. People found beauty, harmony, and unity in nature, for instance, in what they called the great chain of being, from God down—angels, animals, fish, insects, plants, stones, and minerals—everything has a purpose. Hugh of St. Victor said, "Every [living] nature tells of God; every nature teaches man; every nature reproduces its essential form, and nothing in the universe is infecund."[3] He found beauty in numbers: for example, in multiplying by three, every fourth number ends in one (3, 9, 27, 81 . . .). This, he said, was a code God planted in the universe; in this case it affirmed the three Persons of the Trinity and their oneness. Scripture was like a beautiful lock; it could be opened using the right keys, such as the classic four "senses" of Scripture that G. R. Evans identifies as the foundation of all medieval biblical interpretation.[4]

For the people of that time, all scripture testifies to its unity, namely Christ. Even the notion that some people were not intended to understand scripture (Isa 6:9-10) was testimony to the beauty of God's overall plan. Simple meanings in one place of the Bible help unlock more complex meanings in other places. Nature was also in code that one could unlock with scripture. Understanding God's intended meaning of scripture, one could read nature for its own witness to the unity and purpose of the Creator.

General Guidelines for Preachers to Speak of Beauty Today

What has changed? What might need to change in our own understandings to speak effectively of beauty in today's world? Culture has moved away from the great theory of beauty, and this has implications for how preachers speak of it:

(1) Be cautious using the word *beauty.* Beauty is now subjective and cultural, not objective and universal. When novelist Margaret Wolfe Hungerford wrote in *Molly Bawn* (1878), "beauty is in the eyes of the beholder," she opposed people in her day thinking it was a fixed standard. Beauty is now not only subjective but also a matter of cultural conditioning and interpretation; it has to do with context and perspective. *Beauty* can be a

sexist term applied to women, reinforcing cultural stereotypes. A picture of a beautiful funnel cloud on the prairies may be horrifying to someone who has experienced a tornado. A tattoo may be beautiful but for some it symbolizes gang violence. In Korea and Taiwan, a traditional fish dish lives up to its translated name, "stinky tofu," but those who love it find the taste beautiful. Jean-François Lyotard speaks with appropriate nuance: beauty "appeals to the principle of a universal consensus (which may never be attained)."[5]

(2) Be cautious using the word *unity* that often goes hand in hand with *beauty.* Be careful in naming where unity exists. The medieval unity of all things is gone. The unity of the Bible is gone: Scholars have identified many authors, editors, and social situations that influenced its demise. The biblical theology movement in the mid-twentieth century collapsed when it failed to identify unifying themes. Unity of meaning and interpretation is gone. There are differing versions of history, many kinds of lenses with which Scripture can be read (e.g., feminist, black, Min Jung, postcolonial), and many cultural and experiential perspectives of today's readers. Unity, understood as *good,* is dead in many places. Many historians have presented a unified vision of history and have thereby silenced the voices of the poor and powerless.

(3) Avoid assuming fixed standards of beauty. Beauty comes into existence in being perceived. A definition of beauty from 1969 is dated: "the quality present in a thing or person giving intense pleasure or deep satisfaction to the mind."[6] An editor today might use a red pencil on, "the quality present in a thing or person." Beauty no longer exists in things or people; it is a quality attributed by the perceiver. Something becomes beautiful while engaging with it, in the act of perception. Beauty has no singular quality the world over; cultures vary; teenagers and grandparents do not necessarily agree on beauty. The words, "giving intense pleasure or deep satisfaction to the mind," imply that beauty is never disturbing. The Lockheed Martin F-35 Lightning II fighter plane is beautiful engineering but is also disturbing as a huge expense and possible instrument of death. Beauty does not just appeal to "the mind," it has to do with values and matters emotional, kinesthetic, intuitive, and spiritual.

(4) Speak of beauty not least in terms of relationships. Beauty emerges out of them. The ability to find beauty in life largely depends on having good relationships. Acknowledge that beauty changes in the course of a relationship, for instance, through getting to know someone better and appreciation deepening. When Craig Barnes dedicates his book, "For my wife, Dawne, the morning light beside me on the porch," he speaks of rich love

based in fond rituals over time, comparing Dawne's beauty to the rising day.[7] Beauty is fluid because perceptions of beauty change. In troubled relationships, the partner who was attractive a few months ago may seem so no longer because of what he or she has done. Business recognizes the fluid nature of beauty, hence it promotes fashion and consumption.

On the other hand, first, beauty has not necessarily changed as much as some scholars suggest, at least from a Christian perspective. For preachers, the primary focus for beauty is people in relation to God and creation. Most contemporary philosophers leave God out of discussions of beauty. Beauty for them has only momentary life in perception and memory. However, if one understands God to be the source of all beauty, goodness, and truth, then beauty has a life beyond our own limited individual perceptions. Beauty is found wherever the Holy Spirit is encountered; at home, in the church, in the world, and for many who think in theological terms, in the relationship of the three Persons of the Trinity.

For preachers, the primary focus for beauty is people in relation to God and creation.

Second, beauty as unity is still possible. Granted that worldviews today are fragmentary and do not apply equally to all. Granted there can be real danger in imposing on others a worldview that falsely invokes unity and stresses conformity. Nonetheless, a thoughtful and discerning faith still can give testimony to one God and the beauty of God's promises. God's unity is not singular—a notion that defies math yet is coherent in poetry. Unity exists as God's love and purpose over against chaos and destruction. This unity penetrates and ultimately transforms the effects of sin and evil, the destruction of the planet by human endeavor, war, and natural disasters, and the ongoing suffering of so many individuals and communities.

Preachers in the modern era could praise God's beauty and expect assent. Today that might seem to listeners like the wishful thinking of a greeting card in blind ignorance of the news. The best strategy for preachers may be to show dual simultaneous awareness of both beauty and its opposites. Ed Farley argues that redemption brings a deeper sensitivity to beauty and harmony, and simultaneously, a deeper awareness of its opposite, the tragic and chaotic.[8] In other words, lack of unity in the moment does not remove a larger sense of unity and purpose.

In the remainder of this chapter we turn to what the Bible says about beauty, and initial steps preachers may follow in employing it.

Letting the Bible Teach Preachers about Beauty

Gerard Manley Hopkins describes the beauty of God's plan: "The world is charged with the grandeur of God. / It will flame out, like shining from shook foil. / It gathers to a greatness."[9] Our own words need not be so magnificent, but we might nonetheless learn from those for whom God's beauty has been central, and we might look for inspiration to poets like Maya Angelou, Mary Oliver, Wendell Berry, Billy Collins, James Weldon Johnson, Gerard Manley Hopkins, Langston Hughes, Margaret Avison, and more. Our interest is how the sermon can appeal to beauty, and better testify to the beauty of God. Yet what better place to look than to the beauty of the biblical words? As models for us, they suggest ways preaching can be more beautiful.

Simone Weil, philosopher and mystic, observed that most people find their way to God through beauty, yet Christian tradition says very little about this.[10] Indeed, *beauty* is not a common word in the Bible. The psalmist speaks of God's beauty, "I have asked one thing from the Lord— / it's all I seek: / to live in the Lord's house all the days of my life, / seeing the Lord's beauty / and constantly adoring his temple" (Ps 27:4). God alludes to the land and salvation as beautiful, "How wonderful it would be / to treat you like children / and give you a beautiful land, / an inheritance unrivaled among the nations" (Jer 3:19). The feet of those who proclaim the gospel are said to be beautiful (Isa 52:7; Rom 10:14).

Often biblical writers describe beautiful things in beautiful ways without using the word *beautiful.* Various Hebrew words connected with God's glory (e.g., *kabod, hadar,* and *hod*) have an aesthetic dimension though they point to God's strength, splendor, or honor. We do the same thing with words like *awesome, amazing, stunning, brilliant,* and so on; they carry aesthetic weight. Critics might say beauty is impressionistic, and they are right. At the same time, beauty is not a matter of free-for-all, and any serious conversation about it must be able to explain itself. Like preaching, beauty is not objective; it is testimony, witness, confession, which makes it well-suited for preaching. The Bible is not all sweetness and light, which is why beauty must be assessed in context, in relation to what it counters.

In specific, how might preachers speak about beauty in their own sermons?

(1) Preachers may turn for guidance to what the biblical writers found beautiful.

(2) Preachers may look to what they themselves find beautiful in the biblical witnesses. Even if the biblical writer does not write of beauty, a preacher may find the writer's description beautiful. In this we may find more beauty in the Bible than we can exhaust with a lifetime of preaching.

(3) Preachers need not insist that others must see beauty as they see it. We speak to the beauty we find in the hope that others may be similarly arrested, captivated, inspired, or renewed.

Categories of Biblical Beauty for Preaching

Beauty is the source of knowledge for Aristotle because people want to know beauty better. Most Christians find aspects of their faith profoundly beautiful, though they seldom speak of it. Beauty in the modern era was often associated with superficial things, like feelings, emotions, and outward appearances. The power of beauty to draw people to faith was underestimated. God as the source of true beauty has also been overlooked. Preachers should not look for what would be universally agreed as beautiful, but rather find what they or their community of faith might find beautiful. Once there, preachers may tap into a source of passion.

Here are several categories upon which preachers might focus: the beauty of creation, God's actions and character, the person and works of Jesus Christ, the ongoing work of the Spirit, and the voice of God in the present.

The Beauty of Creation

How might we as preachers speak to the beauty of creation, beyond acknowledging that creation is fallen? I am captivated by the Kepler telescope, now wobbling uncontrollably in space and unable to focus. It has enabled astronomers to predict in "one lowball estimate" that there may be as many as 17 billion planets similar to Earth in just the Milky Way, planets with "just the right conditions for life."[11] I find that possibility both amazing and wonderful, and I would use that in a sermon to speak of the mystery and grandeur of God. I find similar wonder and beauty in the accounts of Christmas—that the God of the universe would care so much as to become human for us.

Preachers may speak of *the beauty of creation in relation to God.* Genesis 1 speaks of the six days of creation, and each day describes something of great beauty that God calls "good" and "supremely good" (1:31): day one, the heavens and earth, light and darkness; day two, the dome of sky and the waters; day three, the sea and land with "plants yielding seeds, each according to its kind, and trees bearing fruit with seeds inside it, each according to its kind" (1:12); day four, the sun, moon, and stars; day five, the fish and birds, "the great sea animals and all the tiny living things that swarm in the waters, each according to its kind, and all the winged birds" (1:21); day six, the land creatures, "every kind of living thing: livestock, crawling things, and wildlife" (1:24), and humanity in the image of God (1:26). The point here is praising God. Speak of the beauty of creation not just when we preach on Genesis, but in any sermon.

Similar testimonies are found in the psalms, where "glory" is often associated with light and with the majesty and greatness of God. Psalm 19 says that the heavens declare God's glory, "there's no speech, no words— / their voices can't be heard— / but their sound extends throughout the world; / their words reach the ends of the earth" (vv. 3-4). Psalm 29 praises storms: "the glorious God thunders; / the Lord is over the mighty waters. / The Lord's voice is strong; / the Lord's voice is majestic" (vv. 3-4). Psalm 104 speaks in beautiful ways of God setting limits on the waters (v. 9) and of tending creation on a daily basis: "All your creations wait for you / to give them their food on time. / When you give it to them, they gather it up; / when you open your hand, they are filled completely full!" (vv. 27-28.) When we as preachers find ourselves speaking of creation, might we become more hymnic in praise?

Beauty in spite of hardship. Of course in our own age we tend to hear such testimony with a loud "yes but." We remember all of the people who do not get food on time. Many put the blame on God, rather than human greed. In Job 38-41, God speaks out of the whirlwind, in plain awareness of all of the tragic loss that Job has experienced. The issue of suffering is not resolved in the text, but it puts things in a theological perspective that has appeal:

> who laid [the earth's] cornerstone,
> while the morning stars sang in unison
> and all the divine beings shouted?
> Who enclosed the Sea behind doors

> when it burst forth from the womb,
> when I made the clouds its garment,
> the dense clouds its wrap,
> when I imposed my limit for it,
> put on a bar and doors
> and said, 'You may come this far, no farther;
> here your proud waves stop'?" (38:6-11)

Beauty exists in nature not in absence of natural disasters and tragedies, yet somehow in spite of them. The best funeral services do not stay with suffering and loss, but move to beauty and hope beyond the present moment.

God's Actions and Character as Beauty

God's saving and sustaining actions are beautiful. Sometimes just the occasional words are enough to generate an impression of God's beauty. For instance, when speaking of God acting in the present, preachers might pause to admire the beauty of it.

Jeremy Begbie speaks of the beauty of "the Creator's faithful *commitment* to the cosmos" in its "otherness."[12] Isaiah and Paul identify God's saving acts, the "gospel", as beautiful. Even brief commentary can point to the beauty of God: "awesome deeds" (Ps 65:5) of deliverance and sustenance cause people on the edges to "stand in awe of your acts" (65:8). Listen to the psalmist's exuberance: "your paths overflow with rich food. / Even the desert pastures drip with it, / and the hills are dressed in pure joy. / The meadowlands are covered with flocks, / the valleys decked out in grain— / they shout for joy; / they break out in song!" (Ps 65:11-13). In our own time, might not we praise creation in such lavish and beautiful ways? Perhaps, mainly at Thanksgiving, do we come close.

God's character is beautiful. God's character is revealed in God's actions, notably the Exodus. Moses is inspired to sing (and Miriam to dance and sing), "Who is like you among the gods, Lord? / Who is like you, foremost in holiness, / worthy of highest praise, doing awesome deeds?" (Exod 15:11). The psalmist recites the trials Israel has been through and ends praising God for being faithful, "But God definitely listened. / He heard the sound of my prayer. / Bless God! He didn't reject my prayer; / he didn't withhold his faithful love from me" (66:19-20). Throughout the Bible, God's holiness, perfection, faithfulness, justice, steadfast love, and providence are praised. God "will not allow you to be tempted beyond your abilities" and "will also supply a way out so that you will be able to endure it" (1 Cor 10:13).

The future belongs to God and is beautiful. Preachers tend rarely, except at funerals, to speak of the end times, much less to attribute beauty to it. There is beauty in an age to come, for instance in Isaiah 66:18-19: "I'm coming to gather all nations and cultures. They will come to see my glory. I will put a sign on them.... They will declare my glory among the nations."

The event of salvation has astounding beauty. The "Lord's glory" shines around the shepherds at Christ's birth (Luke 2:9); the second coming of the Son of Man will be in glory (Matt 16:27; see: Mark 8:38; 1 Pet 4:13); believers will share in his glory (1 Cor 15: 43; Rev 19:7; 21:22-26). Salvation happens in the past (Eph 2:5, 8), present (we who are "being saved" in 1 Cor 1:18; 15:2), and future ("we will be saved" Rom 5:9-10; 1 Cor 5:5; Ephesians 2:7)—three ways preachers might embrace, as Paul does in his beautiful words, "I'm convinced that nothing can separate us from God's love in Christ Jesus our Lord: not death or life, not angels or rulers, not present things or future things, not powers or height or depth, or any other thing that is created" (Rom 8:38-39).

The Person and Works of Jesus Christ as Beauty

Beauty extends to Christ, as is reflected in the great hymn "Fairest Lord Jesus": "All fairest beauty heavenly and earthly, / wondrously, Jesus, is found in Thee; / none can be nearer, fairer or dearer / than Thou, my Savior, art to me." Isaiah 53:2 says of the Suffering Servant that, "He possessed no splendid form for us to see, / no desirable appearance." His beauty is of a different sort. His glory is preexistent, "before the creation of the world" (John 17:24). At the end of time he comes in glory (Matt 16:27; Mark 8:38). John writes of a different kind of beauty, he is "full of grace and truth" (1:14). The author of Colossians says, "All the treasures of wisdom and knowledge are hidden in him" (2:3) and he is "the image of the invisible God" (1:15). His authority and power to forgive sins are reasons to give God glory (Matt 9:5-8). His signs reveal his glory (John 2:11). In his transfiguration, his "face shone like the sun" (Matt 17:2) and "his clothes were amazingly bright, brighter than if they had been bleached white" (Mark 9:3). In the Gospel of John, the cross represents Jesus's hour of glorification, for the world has done its worst and is unable to defeat him (12:23). In the Synoptic Gospels, the resurrection at Easter is the time of glory, reflected in the dawn and the dazzling appearance of the angels (Matt 28:3; Luke 24:4).

It is relatively easy to discover God's beauty in rainbows and butterflies, mountain vistas and waterfalls. It is harder for us to see beauty in the cross as an instrument of torture, yet there is beauty in the love that inspired Jesus's total self-giving. Perhaps as preachers who follow a Christ who calls us to *kenosis* and loss, we can model finding beauty in less, in the emptying, in the fast, even (though it is hard) in the loss or in grief, particularly if in it we are assured of Christ's presence in the Spirit. We often find in parishioners a desire to equate the "beautiful" with the "pleasant." But many experiences, circumstances, and people reveal the beauty of God at work in less-than-pleasant ways, often in the midst of suffering or the presence of death. We might speak of Christ's love passionately, in these circumstances, as Augustine did in his *Confessions,* "Late have I loved you, beauty so old and so new: late have I loved you. And see, you were within and I was in the external world and sought you there. . . . You were with me, and I was not with you."[13]

We often find in parishioners a desire to equate the "beautiful" with the "pleasant."

Paul finds beauty in the gospel message ("How beautiful are the feet...", Rom 10:15) that he centers in the resurrection through preaching (1 Cor 1:17-18). This power is not abstract and unseen, but visible transformation of the lives of the hearers. He finds beauty in the mystery of Christ, for he revels, "God's riches, wisdom, and knowledge are so deep! They are as mysterious as his judgments. / Who has known the Lord's mind?" (Rom 11:33-34). Paul contrasts the "wisdom that comes from the present day" with "God's wisdom" from "before time began" that God reveals "for our glory" (1 Cor 2:6-7). Christ himself is praised as "the Lord of glory" (1 Cor 2:8) and "the wisdom from God" (1 Cor 1:30). In Christ, Paul seems to find a cosmic beauty: "Therefore, God highly honored him / and gave him a name above all names, / so that at the name of Jesus everyone / in heaven, on earth, and under the earth might bow / and every tongue confess that / Jesus Christ is Lord, to the glory of God the Father" (Phil 2:9-11).

The Ongoing Work of the Spirit as Beauty

Another category of beauty preachers may consider is the ongoing work of the Spirit, particularly the life and work of the church. Hymn writers have been alert to this, as in "Jesu, Joy of Our Desiring," which speaks of the beauty and wisdom in community experience, "where the flock, in you confiding, / drink of joy from deathless springs. / Theirs is beauty's fairest pleasure; / theirs is wisdom's holiest treasure. / You, forever, lead your own in the love of joys unknown." In the Bible, God gives sun and rain to "the evil and the good" alike (Matt 5:45), yet there are some gifts the Spirit gives only to the church (1 Pet 4:11), such as authority to make disciples (Matt 28:18-20). As preachers, if we find that beautiful, might we not speak of it?

Of course there can be danger in attributing beauty too readily, partly because of the Fall, without giving sufficient evidence of what exactly we find beautiful. For instance, Paul says that glory shines through the life of the church "from one degree of glory to the next" (2 Cor 3:18; see 1 Cor 11:7). Today that can be heard as triumphalistic and off-putting unless it is placed within the context of Paul's thought. We can speak more readily of the Spirit empowering believers to beautiful acts: of holiness (1 Cor 6:18-20), obedience (2 Cor 9:13), generosity (2 Cor 9:13) good deeds (1 Pet 2:11-12), suffering for others (Rom 8:17-18), prayer (John 14:13); love and unity (John 17:27); faith and confidence (Rom 4:20). As Paul says, "All of God's promises have their yes in him. That is why we say Amen through him to the glory of God" (2 Cor 1:20).

The gifts of the Spirit are beautiful. They are variously identified: Romans 12:6-8 lists prophecy, service, teaching, encouragement, giving, leadership, and mercy; 1 Corinthians 12:8-10 lists wisdom, knowledge, faith, healing, miracles, prophecy, tongues, and interpretation of tongues. James 1:17 presents a simpler approach, "Every good gift, every perfect gift, comes from above." We as preachers could do more to speak of the beauty of the gifts God offers. In the current age we tend to think that we as human beings are the source of knowledge, as though the truths of science are our creation. Proverbs knows differently; wisdom and knowledge are from God (Prov 2:6) and promises, "Wisdom will enter your mind, / and knowledge will fill you with delight. / Discretion will guard you; / understanding will protect you. / Wisdom will rescue you from the evil path" (2:10-12; see Ps 111:10).

The Voice of God as Beauty

Origen said that when a preacher faithfully preaches the gospel Christ speaks. Christ's words are sacramental; they bear God to the people; God uses them to commune with us. More than information *about* something, these words do what they say. The preacher, on behalf of God, says the words of a loving parent to willing children. The people experience these words of proclamation as a form of personal address from God. Perhaps the words are from a particular biblical text, not necessarily the preaching text, for example, "Don't fear, because I am with you; / don't be afraid, for I am your God. / I will strengthen you, / I will surely help you; / I will hold you / with my righteous strong hand" (Isa 41:10). Perhaps the words are of Jesus to the woman caught in adultery, "Neither do I condemn you. Go, and from now on, don't sin anymore" (John 8:11). The sermon builds to such words; they need the right context and timing; good teaching precedes them, but when they come, they come as words that focus what has been said. They come as the "I" speech of God to "you" as God's people. Folks may experience them as words of grace that meet their specific needs that day. Hearing God speak directly to one's need can be the most beautiful thing because it places one in the arms of a loving God.

To speak on behalf of God in this manner is a bold thing, some would say too bold. On the other hand, who does anything less bold simply by standing in the pulpit? The people listen not only for a word about God but also listen for God. These words cast people not on their own resources, but on God's power. Such words of the gospel are the heart of the Bible.[14] Isaiah says of God, "my word that comes from my mouth; / it does not return to me empty. / Instead, it does what I want, / and accomplishes what I intend" (55:11). If Paul is right, gospel words are uttered in the power of the resurrection, and bear with them not only the brokenness of the cross but also the new life that ends the old creation and begins the new. They are the ultimate words of beauty, goodness, and truth. They have power beyond this age, beyond all intellectual power of reason and understanding. Gospel words are performing words, action words of beauty, goodness, and truth.

Resistance to Preaching and Beauty

Preachers have not been accustomed to think of their task in terms of beauty. We do not typically sit down to prepare a sermon and say, "I will craft something beautiful." We may not think the congregation expects to hear something beautiful. We may not think, "I have something beautiful to give." And we may not think that the Holy Spirit seeks to provide a beautiful experience. Beauty may seem like a frill. When we stand in front of the word bin marked, "Adjectives for Good Preaching," we tend to reach for *biblical, faithful, doctrinal, theological, relevant, ethical, challenging, helpful, inspiring*, or *creative.* Beauty is often in a bin marked "Arts and Entertainment." Zwingli and Calvin feared lest anything get in the way of God's solemn instruction yet they would not object to the beauty of scripture. Beauty could still be found even in Calvin's churches, but it was the spare beauty of sung psalms, unadorned architecture, and the plain style of preaching.

Perhaps some preachers are reluctant to think of their work as beauty because they have inherited modern notions of beauty as entertainment, or as feminine, or as somehow related to sexuality and posing dangers, or as a universal standard that has had a negative impact on many people. Postmodern attitudes towards beauty depart from the modern. They affect how we think of the beauty of preaching.

1. Beauty has moral complexity.

Beauty ought not to be talked about from the pulpit as though it is automatically good. Young people are encouraged by our culture to pursue beauty as the meaning and purpose of life, often at great cost to their emotional and physical well-being. Beauty is often a commodity. Howard Gardner notes that, "Beauty is based on a hierarchy that labels some things undeniably 'beautiful' and others irretrievably ugly."[15] Beauty also can be for good, and preachers need to be alert to both the dangers and the advantages of appealing to it.

2. Preaching can be too poetic.

When preaching becomes too "beautiful," and words become too carefully crafted, too literary, the words draw attention away from the Word. Not everyone in the congregation can follow imagery. Weary of a rich fare and too many poetic associations, listeners may feel overstimulated, befuddled, or left behind. Most people need a logical development of the sermon, whether in narrative, point, or hybrid form. The beauty the preacher should be most concerned to provide is the beauty of God in saving and empowering action.

3. Preaching is more than harmony.

Beauty is often associated with harmony and some preachers may associate beauty in sermons with making everything harmonious, ignoring discord and trouble. To reduce preaching to this kind of harmony means that preaching loses its character as a gospel word that challenges and overturns the world. Jeremy Begbie cautions that harmonious models of creation fail to take account of the unpredictability of creation and the irrationality of evil. Beauty does not flow automatically but is in relation to what God is doing at this specific moment in creation.[16] The Word of God brings people to a change of heart or behavior. When Jesus says he is to "preach good news to the poor, / to proclaim release to the prisoners / and recovery of sight to the blind, / to liberate the oppressed" (Luke 4:18), his words are not good news for the status quo. The Word is two-edged, it tears down and raises up, condemns and restores, binds and liberates. The harmony that preachers uphold is not the status quo; it is the unity of all in Christ's love and purpose.

4. Beauty may domesticate preaching.

Beauty is not the primary purpose of the sermon; communicating a living relationship with God is the goal, at least to my way of thinking. William Carl Placher wrote *The Domestication of Transcendence*, in which he critiques the modern period for attempting "to subject the divine to the structures of human reason."[17] He says, "before the seventeenth century, most Christian theologians were struck by the mystery, the wholly otherness of God, and the inadequacy of any human categories as applied to God."[18] Beauty would domesticate God if it became a goal in itself rather than a value that emerges in service of God.

Why Beauty Now for Preaching

We may speak here of two levels of beauty. The first, beauty 1, is popular notions of beauty, largely separate from notions of God. It is largely sensory, and its perception may be largely spontaneous and preanalytical. The second level, beauty 2, is connected explicitly with God. Beauty is seen not only in relation to God, but also almost from the perspective of God, creation conforming to God's will and desire. This level may contradict the world: For instance, the inner character of people best determines beauty. Ideally in each sermon, there is a movement to beauty 2. Each sermon enacts the new creation.

What are the benefits of increased attention to beauty?

(1) People long for beauty. Most people I know take vacations in beautiful places, not gravel pits. They ask for rooms with a view, not views of a brick wall. When people describe themselves as "spiritual not religious," they often mean they long for experiences of beauty. Beauty can provide a significant way for the church to connect to diverse people from diverse backgrounds. The church has much to learn from the arts, like how better to communicate the world as it often is. And the church has much to teach the world about deeper, richer understandings of beauty.

(2) When beauty is conceived as of God, the focus of sermon writing shifts. The preacher's task shifts beyond the mere exposition of a particular biblical text, understood as a unit or pericope of scripture, to also expounding the coherence and unity of faith. It is possible to preach most biblical texts, even following the commentary of some biblical scholars, and not get to God or the gospel. The good news is beautiful, and when that becomes the goal of preaching, preachers look for intertextual connections, links to key events in Jesus's story, to reinforce the good news found in the text at hand. In other words, preaching should preach the text within the larger picture of the faith, with the cross and Easter in focus to remind hearers of the heart of the faith. This vision of the whole points to the beauty of God's world, and goodness and justice within it.

(3) Beauty, and theopoetics in general, is a reaction to preaching that is excessively addressed to reason. Christian doctrines/traditional teachings are essential; they are ways to condense what the scriptures say; they are ways to make sense of diverse biblical texts and understandings; they present the faith as a kind of whole. They may even have beauty at times, but when presented as yes or no, without connection to their biblical roots, they can lead people away from scripture and the kind of fresh encounter with God that is the gospel. Doctrines as propositions tend to invoke authority from ecclesial or other sources, instead of locating authority in the community encounter with God's Word.

(4) Beauty offers listeners a fresh perspective. They often tune out when they feel they have heard something before. Studies indicate that, "whenever a sight or sound becomes familiar, individuals avert their eyes or tune out. And, as a contrast, when deviations from the 'new norm' emerge, these attract attention instead, unless they have become so complex that they cannot be assimilated."[19] When preachers show beauty in the overfamiliar, the divine in the ordinary, or the holy in the midst of the profane, there is a freshness that commands attention.

(5) An old maxim applies to preaching—less is more. It speaks to economy and favoring understatement to overstatement. Poetry often

conveys its meaning in a tight economy of words. There is a beauty in homiletical economy as well, as I have said elsewhere in advocating elements of sermon unity—ONE text, ONE theme, ONE doctrine (traditional church teaching connected with the text), ONE need (of someone that this sermon addresses), ONE image (i.e., a dominant or repeating image), ONE mission (a possible action that leads from the sermon).[20] This spartan simplicity can be beautiful. In a culture that tends to equate "beauty" with "more," with acquisition and consumption, homiletical economy might be thought of in terms of Calvinist notions of beauty, yet not so much plain as precise. Oftentimes a metaphor is a brilliantly economical way to express a much more complex idea that really just couldn't be explained another way, like Jesus as the Lamb of God. Sermons can have similar kinds of economy as beauty.

(6) Theopoetics encourages people to find beauty in their own story. Companies like Walmart and Amazon have priced many smaller businesses out of the market. There is a trend among consumers to reject the big stores and look for local produce, craft and specialty foods, designs, and the like. These consumers buy not only products but a story and identity. An independent perfume-maker says, "Consumers want self-discovery, and not us trying to dictate some story."[21] Preaching that offers beauty invites self-discovery.

Getting Started

If we preach with beauty in mind, we may be less tempted to rely excessively on reason and the intellect, essential though they are. Here we start at the beginning of the sermon process in naming practical strategies to employ beauty and preaching.

Choose a Simple Idea as the Theme Sentence

Preachers might learn from golf. Joan Vickers, a researcher at the University of Calgary, advocates that golfers improve their game with what she calls the "quiet eye."[22] Some golfers have jumpy eyes, even while swinging. In just a few seconds, they look at the rough, the pond, the tree, the green, the shank of the club, their hands, the ball, their feet. Excellent, experienced putters apparently "quiet" their eyes before they make the swing. They first look at the hole as a way to program the mind where the ball is to go, and then they concentrate on the ball—well, not on the ball itself but the spot of ground right behind it, so the head does not lift to follow the ball. The process ends in greater accuracy. Lifting the head can throw a shot off because follow-through is affected.

As preachers we tend to have jumpy eyes in sermon preparation. We may look at the Bible text, biblical commentaries, websites, journals, newspapers, recent books—all good things—and may never focus on one clear idea. Sunday comes and the preacher in the pulpit takes one wild swing after another. A sermon can be sent into the rough as easily as a golf ball off the tee.

The sermon must say something substantial and make sense; it cannot be a sound and light show of images and ideas. A theme sentence makes a claim and is a complete thought arising from the biblical text, like "Jesus heals the sick" or "God guides Israel." A theme sentence is not a topic like sickness or wealth. A young woman returned from church lamenting the sermon that had been on all Ten Commandments, "It was like listening to a thousand fortune cookies." The preacher had no theme sentence. A theme sentence is the single most important source of unity and hence beauty in a sermon. It needs to be repeated in many ways so people get it. It has to be short so they remember it; five or six words is about right. Good examples may be found from various authors in the *Abingdon Theological Companion to the Lectionary.*[23]

A theme sentence is the single most important source of unity and hence beauty in a sermon.

Having a theme sentence that repeats many times in a sermon, in one way or another, might seem either simplistic or lacking in art. However, this approach is not so much simplistic as simple: Being simplistic or superficial offers no substantial beauty, but being simple often does. Simplicity is not just clarity. It can be elegant.

A theme sentence functions in a sermon much as a focal point functions in a work of art. (Here I am not thinking of classical art, not postmodern art that shuns unity and focus.) Art classes often use the classical golden rule. Artists divide their rectangular canvas into thirds, using vertical and horizontal lines. There will thus be four places where vertical and horizontal lines intersect. Painters are taught to have one of these as the place of focus. They design their works so that the eye naturally moves to that one place, perhaps directed by the shape of a hillside or the angle of a roof. Paintings can have many details, but the whole painting functions as one, much as a sermon should function with a theme sentence. Without one a sermon can sound like a golfer beating through bushes to find a lost ball.

Choose a Beautiful Idea

In the postmodern era, what is practical often rules: Preachers need to be understood, they cannot experiment with new forms that try to disorientate one week, or make listeners angry the next. Choose an idea that strikes you as beautiful to be the focus of your sermon, like "Christ blesses the poor" or "God empowers us to love." God doing something in the biblical text will allow one to speak of the gospel as the good news it is. God as the subject of the theme sentence is key. An image or emotion (like love) may be enough for a sermon title or topic, but is not enough for a theme sentence. Similarly a question is inadequate ("Do you love enough?")—it does not say anything about the subject. What is the sermon actually going to say? An idea is a complete thought that makes a claim. It needs to be a complete sentence (e.g., "God gives the love we share.")

The theme sentence is the lens through which a preacher looks at the text and the world in the week prior to the sermon. It functions like a camera, and if the preacher carries it throughout the week, events will come into focus through it. I once took a photography class. We went out on a cold, wet day in the city, a miserable experience. However, because we were carrying our cameras, we saw things we otherwise would not see. We caught glimpses of rare beauty, like a leak in an old gutter on the corner of a slate roof. A theme sentence is a preacher's camera. It allows a preacher to see beauty by pausing, framing, adjusting the light, finding God acting in so many ways that relate to the sermon at hand. That is what the sermon should do for the listeners: It is a camera they can take out into the world to look for signs of God.

What is beauty in this context? Educator Howard Gardner identifies three qualities that we could adapt to the theme sentence:[24] "The object is interesting; its form is memorable; it invites further encounters."[25]

How might we apply this to a theme sentence?

(a) Interesting: For something to be interesting it must *alter the familiar in some way*. Whatever is said about God must sound fresh, to avoid individuals averting their eyes or tuning out.

(b) Memorable/Embodied: A prerequisite for beauty is memorable form; interest must be "embodied in a form or format *sufficiently powerful or evocative that it will be remembered in that form.*" [26] The theme sentence points to signature actions of God. The stories that one builds around it are memorable. Stories create events; they generate some of the actual experience of God that preachers are concerned to tell.

(c) Invitational of Further Encounters: Gardner speaks of the *desire to revisit the object or the thought,*[27] like a short film he saw of an old typewriter filling up with snow. There was something about watching that film that was beautiful, powerful; every time he saw snow fall he thought of it. The stories a preacher tells can have a similar effect: A woman visited in a senior's residence. In the course of visiting a man whose wife had recently died, she asked if he would like a prayer. She thought she was going to pray but instead he launched into prayer and did so intimately, so beautifully, expressing the same kind of love for God that she imagined him doing with his wife, and it seemed to the woman as though God was right there in the room with them. Such a story in a sermon might create in listeners a desire to revisit God, to hear again what spoke to the heart.

A sermon in theory can be based on any old idea, but making God the subject prevents God from going missing in the rough. Here is an example of choosing a theme sentence: The Prodigal Son in Luke 15:11-32 speaks of the father's love. The theme sentence could be "The father is prodigal (wasteful) with his love." However, because a sermon should do more to explore a biblical text, it should say something about God's gracious action in or behind the text. Thus the theme sentence could be "God's love is wasteful."

To me, this approach to the sermon, early in the week, helps ensure that a preacher speaks not only about love in the biblical text but also connects that love to God. Preaching implies faith, faith implies a relationship with God, and relationships with God empower ministries that can change the world. Churchgoers are blessed when preachers treat the Bible in some way as the Word of God, and speak about God's grace and good news.

Chapter Three

Christmas Strategies for Beauty (Practice)

This chapter for the most part practices theopoetics. It does so in relation to one of the key actions of God in the Bible, namely God's coming in Jesus Christ. In looking at Christmas, and in later chapters at Easter and Pentecost, we look at three key moments in the Christian metanarrative (overarching story), something that is regarded with suspicion in postmodern circles. These are three big gospel celebrations that need to inform weekly preaching much more frequently than often they do. We focus on Christmas as a way to highlight how essential it is, and to help preachers find imaginative ways to conceive of it. We lift up the incarnation as a potential key reference narrative for any sermon at any time of the year. Christmas in particular is about new beginnings and here we look at several new beginnings: beginning the sermon, beginning Jesus's story, the beginning of faith, and the beginning of a new creation.

A Starting Place

The starting place for the sermon is discovering something significant to say early in the week, and then looking for stories to support it.

Theme Sentence

A beautiful sermon begins with an idea that the preacher finds beautiful (i.e., interesting, memorable, and worth revisiting). God needs to be the subject. God doing something in or behind the text is its focus. As a gracious action, it is empowering. It provides the reader with a fresh way to look at something. As I consider the incarnation, I am struck by the potential beauty that may be developed in speaking of a fresh beginning: *God provides a fresh beginning in Christ.* This idea gives only a glimpse of the beauty I see, and that is fine as long as I am clear about it: The sermon is the place to sculpt it. For that I need story.

Sculpting with Story

Some people still think of stories as fiction. More commonly stories are what happen every day. Stories are a way of sharing events, of organizing material, and of communicating not just facts but how events feel. According to Stephen Crites, stories are the way we give order to experience to find meaning in the world.[1] A well-told story actually creates an experience, addresses the senses, allows characters to speak. Therein is the beauty of story: It involves the listeners; it introduces them to real people who actually might speak through the preacher's words; it addresses not just the mind but the whole body and emotions. A good PowerPoint presentation can have its own beauty; it pays attention to what facts are most important, and how best to communicate information. The beauty of story involves paying attention to narrative technique, not to make fiction, but to communicate effectively what we believe to be true. Rather it takes the information at hand and discovers a fresh angle.

Ken Burns is a storyteller whose formula for storytelling is 1 + 1 = 3. "All stories . . . the real genuine stories, are about 1 + 1 = 3."[2] Many people write stories as 1 + 1 = 2, but for a great story, "The whole is greater than its parts. That is the 3."[3] As an example of a great tragic story, he cites Abraham Lincoln winning the Civil War and then finding time to go to the theatre—where of course he is shot and killed. He likes stories that feature good people with flaws or bad people who are compelling. He thinks of Jackie Robinson becoming the first African American player in major league baseball in 1947 when he joined the Brooklyn Dodgers, and he imagines the story of a racist Dodgers fan who has three choices: to give up on baseball, to switch teams, or to change. He looks for stories with conflict or a complication.

How I explain 1 + 1 = 3 might differ from Burns. When I think of a 1 + 1 = 2 story, I think of a story that communicates useful information, but is not very compelling. A woman goes to work and is fired because of downsizing is an = 2 story. It relates an all-too-common, sad event, but it is not very interesting as a story that involves the listener. Of course the story is in the details, but even fleshed out with description and dialogue, it might still lack zip. It needs something else. It is an = 3 story if the woman was going to quit and is angry her boss beat her to it. Or it is an = 3 story if the woman, in returning home early, discovers her husband seriously ill and is able to drive him to hospital. What is that extra element that makes for interest? Sometimes we just need to step back far enough, looking for something that makes for conflict, complication, or surprise. Aristotle thought of plot as involving some sort of reversal in fortune (the woman being fired), or complication (her boss beat her to it), or discovery (saving her husband).[4] For preachers what matters most is to recognize when a third something or element is present in a story, because that makes for magnetic interest.

How to Begin the Sermon Itself

The Synoptic Gospel writers wrote sermons, and each had to wrestle with where to start. Their dilemma is not much different from that of the preacher each week: How will I communicate faith to my people? Each had a concern for beauty. Matthew was a tax collector, so there is beauty to his starting where he does—it is just where a civic official used to record keeping might be expected to start, especially in talking to people versed in Hebrew Scripture, "A record of the ancestors of Jesus Christ, son of David, son of Abraham" (Matt 1:1). He proceeds to provide as complete a genealogy for Jesus as possible. People today who like genealogy might say, "Now is that interesting, Matthew was someone I could relate to," and people living in his time might have found this as well. Paul often gives his own credentials at the beginning of his letters as a way to head off potential critics, and Matthew, in his introduction, does the same thing on behalf of Jesus. He lists some very significant names, and then starts at his true beginning place, "This is how the birth of Jesus Christ took place. When Mary his mother was engaged to Joseph, before they were married, she became pregnant by the Holy Spirit" (1:18). The story of a pregnancy out of wedlock is an = 2 story, but it quickly becomes an = 3 story because of the role of the Holy Spirit.

Mark begins, "The beginning of the good news about Jesus Christ, God's Son" (1:1). He writes to Gentiles who have heard about John the Baptist. In preaching it is important to find something beautiful in the biblical text and portray it as such. I find beauty in how subtly Mark uses prophecy in Isaiah to dismiss the claims of some people in his day that John the Baptist is the Messiah: "[The good news] happened just as it was written about in the prophecy of Isaiah: / *Look, I am sending my messenger before you. / He will prepare your way, / a voice shouting in the wilderness: / 'Prepare the way for the Lord; / make his paths straight*' " (1:2-4). Mark is no-frills and blunt: He has no genealogy or birth narrative; he goes straight to Jesus's ministry. For Mark the descent of the Spirit on Jesus is a more important beginning than his conception or birth. "John the Baptist is not the Messiah" could function as an = 2 story, but Mark makes the story into an = 3: If Jesus is Spirit, John the Baptist is water.

What I especially like about Luke, in contrast to the spare economy of Mark, is the time he takes telling stories. He sets them up. Even the dedication to Theophilus is a way to allow other readers to overhear (a) that he has "investigated everything carefully from the beginning" (1:3), as one might expect of a learned physician, and (b) that what follows is "a carefully ordered account for you . . . to have confidence in the soundness of the instruction you have received" (1:3-4). The opening is a way of giving his credentials, as he presents his concern for truth ("so that you may know the truth concerning the things about which you have been instructed" 1:4 NRSV). Dedication completed, Luke sets the story of Jesus up with Zechariah and Elizabeth unable to conceive. Again, this fairly common story of couples becomes uncommon (hence = 3) when, in leading worship, an angel visits Zechariah as he offers the incense in worship. Further complexity and beauty is added by his doubt of the angel's message and being struck mute until the birth of their son.

The gospel writers knew that a sermon needs a hook to capture interest. For us the hook may be biblical or cultural. Either way, the introduction begins to address the theme sentence. It makes a promise to listeners: This is where we are going. Like on a bus we are about to board, the theme sentence is above the windshield, announcing our destination.

A Beginning Place for Faith

The worship space is often configured around Christian symbols, the cross, the font, the table, the Bible, the pulpit, and each one arises from scripture and says something about God. Stained glass windows often tell Bible stories; they are visual sermons. Banners offer God's praise. Musical instruments speak of celebration. It is telling there are no mirrors: we come to worship God, not ourselves.

Today it is common for people to speak of having many identities, for instance, as a parent, child, teacher, friend, hiker, and so forth, but central to all can be identity in Christ. Faith begins in relation to God—maybe as just a question, or the hope of an encounter, or out of need. Each Sunday is a new beginning. Preachers cannot give faith, for faith comes from God (Rom 12:3; Heb 12:2). As Paul says, "faith comes from listening. . . by means of Christ's message" (Rom 10:17). We can give testimony, enroll listeners in a story, and do as much as we can to speak people into relationship with God. Think of worshipers as people who have come to enact a story. The story varies each week. It is sad, tragic, lamentable, lonely, and even more powerfully hopeful, grace filled, joyous, loving and just, and the combination makes it beautiful. The preacher's task is to help hearers find their place in that story.

Present a Story for Listeners to Be In

A friend spoke of reading a bedtime story to his nieces, ages three and seven. When he finished, the three-year-old took the storybook and stood on it and cried inconsolably. The friend was distressed. "What's the matter? What's the matter?" It was the seven-year-old who answered, "She wants to be in the story."

Some people like to go to Christmas stores all year around, and others avoid them like a dirty needle on a park bench. But come December, most of us want to be in the story of Christ's birth. It may even represent a kind of longing in much of society, a wish to believe that there is a God who really does care about us. But exactly where in the story do we belong?

Preachers invite people to find their own roles by involving them in good storytelling. In Luke, do we as listeners want to be Mary or Joseph as night falls on the journey, chilled with the dampness, worried that darkness will come before they arrive, worried that Mary will go into labor at any moment, worried that if they go any faster the ride will be too rough, worried about where they will stay? Listeners don't always choose their identity in a story; in a way the story chooses them, it names some aspect of who they are. That is what makes stories so powerful.

Alternatively, we may be onlookers cheering for them as underdogs. Or perhaps the plot intrigues us and no matter how many times we have heard it, we want to hear again how this journey ends up: We imagine being with Mary and Joseph at the inn, being told, "Be gone with you, there is no room here." Sometimes imagination is necessary when biblical texts are "fraught with background,"[5] as Eric Auerbach once described that Abraham and Isaac story, and when few textual details are provided. Depending on how we imagine the story, we may identify with the innkeeper in having no room for Mary and Joseph at this time of the year. Or perhaps we imagine a kindly innkeeper who has just started to close the door on them, "Be gone," when she notices, "Oh my dear, you are with child. We have no rooms but we can give you shelter and some clean hay to lie on out in the stable." No sooner are Joseph and Mary settled than Mary goes into labor, in a stall. Perhaps we identify with giving birth.

Preachers need to affirm whatever identity people find in a biblical story. Even if we might be tempted to judge an identity negatively (perhaps the innkeeper who has no time for Christmas), it is nonetheless a starting place in a relationship with God, and that can always be beautiful. Who among us does not need some improvements of the very sort Christmas provides?

One reason so many people like the infancy narrative is what it says about God. This God loves people so much as to become human. Not everyone who comes to church believes the story; some fondly remember Christmases of childhood and at least fantasize about believing now as they did then. Some people see Mary as just another teen pregnancy, but as insiders, we know differently. What makes this story 1 + 1 = 3 is our knowledge of the child's identity. We know the gender of this baby before he is born, and from Matthew we know his lineage and divine conception. Mark tells us the baby is prophesied by Isaiah and will baptize with the Holy Spirit (1:8). We know from Luke he is the Savior born to all people, the prince of peace. These enriching echoes from other parts of scripture are poetic. The contrast between Jesus's identity as "Savior, who is the Messiah, the Lord" (Luke 2:11 NRSV) and his birthplace is part of the intrigue. We know what will happen to him: He will work mighty miracles, speak lasting truths, go the cross to die our death, be raised from the dead, sit at God's right hand, and return again at the end of time to fulfill all divine promises. In fact, the only reason we pay attention to this Bethlehem story, and the only reason it has been preserved as scripture is that it is God's answer to all the trouble in the world and all the trouble we are in.

A fifteenth-century painting by Fra Angelico in the San Marco Museum in Florence, Italy, is entitled "Madonna with the Child, Saints and Crucifixion." Mary is dressed in blue and holds her baby on her lap as she sits on an altar chair, and around her stand nine saints of the church. In the background is a medieval evergreen forest. In the foreground one of the saints looks away from mother and child toward us, the viewers, and he has an expression of profound sadness on his face. At his feet is a small painting facing the viewer, and this picture within the picture is of Jesus on the cross at his crucifixion and two women standing on either side looking up. Angelico's painting makes an important statement. The cross is never far from the crèche.

Present a Story to Be in Us

We have not just the opportunity to be in the story, but for the story to be in us, to guide and shape us. More, we have an opportunity to experience God in the text acting in our lives, and that is a beautiful and wondrous thing. Preaching places people in relationship with God, and preachers start by honoring whatever that relationship is—be it faithful, off-and-on, distant, negative, angry, or nonexistent. Preachers help the biblical story take root in the lives of the hearers. They should hear the text as being not just about others, but about themselves. God's loving actions in the text are God's action now. The story needs to be in them.

The words preached by Horace Bushnell in the mid-1800s seem written for today:

> And the reason why Jesus cannot find room for His gospel is closely analogous to that which He encountered in His birth—viz., that men's hearts are preoccupied.... It is now as then, and then as now; the selfishness and self-accommodation, the coarseness, the want of right sensibility, the crowding, eager state of men, in a world too small for their ambition—all these preoccupy the inn of their affections, leaving only the stable, or some by-place, in their hearts, as little worthy of His occupancy and the glorious errand on which He comes. See how it was with Him in His life.... He came unto His own, and His own received Him not. He was never accepted as a guest of the world, any more than on that first night in the inn. There was not room enough in the world's thought and feeling to hold Him or even to suffer so great a presence, and He was finally expelled.[6]

Bushnell's people are too preoccupied, as indeed we may be, with getting kids to hockey and basketball, with iPads and smartphones, with being the church and trying to keep the fundraisers going. Preachers might put Bushnell's words in the positive, as a kind of vision of what God is accomplishing in this birth, "A day is coming when our hearts will be open... the selfishness and self-accommodation gone," and so on.

Make a strong claim on behalf of God. That is key and that is why the theme sentence focuses on a key action of God in the biblical text. It is surprising how difficult it is for some preachers to make this kind of claim. Maybe they are worried about distorting the Bible if the text does not mention God. Or maybe it is as one person said, "It's all about God." That may well be true, but still, why is God not mentioned in some sermons? Even preachers may resist the story. For some people it can be embarrassing to believe that God became human in a specific human being, to profess a God who intervenes in human life, to speak of a virgin birth, or of angels appearing. If the story is not in us as hearers, then we can push it away.

Martin Buber related this Hassidic tale:

> A rabbi was asked to tell a story. "A story," he said, "must be told in such a way that it constitutes help in itself." And he told: "My grandfather was lame. Once they asked him to tell a story about his teacher. And he related how the Holy Baal Shem used to hop and dance while he prayed. My grandfather rose as he spoke, and he was so swept away by his story that he himself began to hop and dance to show how the master had done. From that hour on he was cured of his lameness. That's the way to tell a story!"[7]

Buber understood about the beauty of a story being in us.

Preach to Lead Others to Witness

Worship leads to witness. The first reference to worship in the New Testament is in Matthew 2:2, when the Wise Men seek from Herod the birthplace of "the king of the Jews" for they "have come to worship him" (NIV, *proskyneo*). There are no Wise Men in Luke, only shepherds who go to see what the angels announced, and they show us what is an ideal response to divine encounter, "The shepherds returned home, glorifying and praising God for all they had heard and seen. Everything happened just as they had been told" (2:20). They were not just in the story; the story was in them, and they shared it with others.

A woman went with her grown daughter to church last Christmas and the minister, she said, seemed to feel bad about having an opinion. Even the daughter who had long since left the church was embarrassed by the service, "Was he apologizing that Jesus was born?" she asked. How much better it is when the Christmas story is inside of us and we tell the story as a mystery into which listeners might enter, a mystery that helps us make sense of the world, that defines who we are, a story without which we could not easily do without. This is the story that God does not despise the lowly, that God assists them on their journey. We ought to tell it with such joy and passion that if we have been stiff in our joints, we find ourselves easily kneeling in worship before this baby; if we are proud, we become humble before a God who loves us so much; if we are disbelieving, we ask God to multiply our small faith; if we are afraid, we take comfort that our Savior will never leave us; if we feel empty, we reach out to others and find that we have something to give. This is not just a story. It is what preachers witness to as our story, our truth, our poetry.

A Beginning We Cannot Control

In the church there is no need to say, "Let's pretend we are in Bethlehem"; we can just go there. The sermon operates with the same notions of time as communion, where right now we gather around the table with all believers, past, present, and future. It is the beauty of poetry. Again this year we will all be there, crowding around the stall in Bethlehem. So much about the season suggests that we are in control. In the early fall the choir begins rehearsing. Come November, someone fetches the crèche scene from the storeroom under the church basement steps, and checks the sheep and the Holy Family for any paint chips and cracks. By Advent someone puts them out on the frozen lawn in the same place where little Timmy Higgins tripped last year and fell into the manger to the amusement of many, new wood marking the crude repair. Other folks assemble the fire-retardant Christmas tree. They decorate it and hang cedar boughs in the foyer. The tree is reminiscent of the tree at Jesus's death, and through our preaching in effect we place on the green branches the ornaments and symbols of our faith, the stories of Jesus's life, work, and promise. The outreach committee organizes Christmas hampers and serves hot meals. And the Christmas Eve services will be like former ones because folks just don't seem to want the heavy metal version of "Away in the Manger."

In church work we partner with God, and it is easy think we are the senior partner. We gather to hear the word and God responds, as though at our beck and call. We get ready for Christmas and it comes. That is our tendency toward math. It can seem like worship is about what we do. The same is true for the Christian year, starting with Advent and Christmas and moving through Epiphany, Lent, Easter, and Pentecost, each year the same. We can think we are the ones in control. Celebrate Christmas and Jesus is born. Celebrate Easter and the resurrection happens. We may never even ask ourselves, "I wonder if Jesus will be born this year? I wonder if Jesus will be raised from the dead?" We count on it. There is no need to mark any of these events if they are not fresh miracles each year, if we do not experience Christ born anew in our hearts, if we do not find faith renewed, not by our doing, but by a new miracle of God through worship in the present. Their beauty comes in being God's events now, in being a new start beyond our control.

The early Monty Python group did a spoof of the BBC news, "This is Avon Adell bringing you news of fresh disasters." When people come to church it should be the reverse, "This is Avon Adell bringing you news of fresh miracles."

Here is an invitation preachers may offer their congregations. Wait on God, seek God's will, discern God's purpose, regain a vision. God's timing is rarely our own. An Episcopal bishop was recently asked, "what are three challenges facing your churches?" and quickly, without even needing to ponder, he responded, (1) declining membership, (2) lack of vision about who we are and what we are to do, and (3) not enough money to start new ministries that we see are needed. The description he offered could apply to many denominations.

> Wait on God, seek God's will, discern God's purpose, regain a vision.

In this time of apparent decline, can we let God be God, can we trust God to bring forth salvation for the church? Jeremiah 18 tells us that God can plant and pluck up and destroy even Israel. We cannot make worship incarnational for others—that is God's work. In the fullness of time, that is, when God decides the time is right, God acts. God may let die our particular expressions of the Christian faith. God is God. On the other hand, we can at the same time act in faith and do as one woman said recently, "When hope runs out, expect resurrection." That is the beauty of God's poetry.

The Beauty of Jesus Christ as the New Beginning

Two paths lead from the stable in Bethlehem, as the magi discovered. One leads back to Herod's palace past shops of glitter and gold, to his killing ways. And the other leads home "by another route" (Matt 2:12). The world might not notice the path that the Magi took if we did not point it out. It is not in the tour guides. It is not well lit, yet at Easter it will be brighter than noonday sun. The path goes to a house where a woman in her eighties lives all alone, with few callers, so few that there is no need for her to get out the Christmas ornaments from the box in the bottom of the cupboard. The path leads to a hospital ward where a young mother lies fearful of surgery, wondering if she will ever wake up to see her children again. It leads to the prison where a man languishes for a murder he does not remember committing. The path leads through graveyards of despair in the Middle East, past a straw hovel in Africa where a woman with AIDS is laying on a mattress, her soon-to-be-orphaned children playing in the dirt floor. The path leads through women's and men's shelters, through the places in your own heart of grief, illness, sin, regret. If this is not where this "other route" leads, this was not the new beginning we thought it was.

We will often witness new beginnings in much the manner of Christ's coming the first time, unobtrusively, inconspicuously. Isaiah said, "A shoot will grow up from the stump of Jesse; / a branch will sprout from his roots" (11:1). A woman recently said, "I have a daughter who is a banker who is addicted to cocaine. I have been praying for her for fifteen years. She has been in and out of rehab clinics, and last week for the first time in all those years, I saw the girl she used to be." In the dimly lit back alleys of Bethlehem and every darkened place, a light comes, as John says, "the light shines in the darkness, / and the darkness doesn't extinguish the light" (1:5). Jesus will be "the true light, which enlightens everyone" (1:9 NRSV), "the light of the world" (8:12).

Christmas traditionally marks Christ's coming in the past, present and future, that is, in his historical birth, in our hearts and minds today, and at the end of time. Math says no one can be born anew each year—Nicodemus must have been reading math the night he later came to Jesus, for he said similar words in wondering how an adult can be born (John 3:4). Not only must we "be born anew" (John 3:7) but also Jesus is born anew in us—how is that possible? All of these rich echoes bouncing between texts, pointing in the same direction, enhance the poetry and the mystery.

Jesus's death marks another new beginning, the new covenant of which Jeremiah spoke, "I will put my Instructions within them and engrave them on their hearts . . . for I will forgive their wrongdoing and never again remember their sins" (31:33, 34). Paul says the same, "you are Christ's letter . . . [not] written on tablets of stone but on tablets of human hearts. . . . He has qualified us as ministers of a new covenant, not based on what is written but on the Spirit" (2 Cor 3:3, 4, 6). Hebrews calls Jesus, "the mediator of the new covenant" (12:24). In our baptism we enter his death and new life. As Romans puts it, "we were buried together with him through baptism into his death, so that just as Christ was raised from the dead through the glory of the Father, we too can walk in newness of life" (6:4).

There is yet more: Every moment is a new beginning, for Jesus says, "Look! I'm making all things new" (Rev 21:5). Paul's words resonate: "If anyone is in Christ, that person is part of the new creation. The old things have gone away, and look, new things have arrived!" (2 Cor 5:17). Physical death is also a new beginning, for Jesus says, "In my Father's house there are many dwelling places. If it were not so, would I have told you that I go to prepare a place for you?" (John 14:2 NRSV).

Jesus was present at the beginning of time. John tells us, "The Word was with God in the beginning. / Everything came into being through the Word, / and without the Word / nothing came into being" (1:2-3). And at the end of time, Jesus says the Son of Man will be coming in a cloud "with power and great glory" (Luke 21:27 NRSV). The Second Coming is yet another new beginning, for there will be "a new heaven and a new earth, for the former heaven and the former earth had passed away, and the sea was no more" (Rev 21:1). Jesus says, "I am the alpha and the omega, the first and the last, the beginning and the end" (Rev 22:13), yet this end is forever newness.

These notions are powerful and fragile; they are carried to us in clay words. These texts reinforce, clarify, mirror, and modify one another. They are poetry. We can try to say it plainer, but we always need to come back to the poem. It is where we begin and end; we cannot do without it, with the One who is the beginning and the end. We cannot say it better. The poem is Christ.

The poem is Christ.

In this section we have begun to consider the impact of postmodernity on preaching. It demands that we rethink our common assumptions and find good reasons to believe what we believe. Preaching can place fresh emphasis on communicating the beauty of God, the beauty of faith, and the beauty of a life lived with God. To do this, sermons need to focus more on God actions and the good news. Postmodernity is suspicious of closed systems of thought and overemphasis on logic and reason, thus sermons also need to be reconceived more as theopoetry than as theologic. Perhaps in doing so we can move from the 1 + 1 = 2 of math to the 1 + 1 = 3 of poetry. We now turn to the second classical value we use to reconceive preaching for our time, and that is the value of goodness.

Part II

Goodness as Relationship

become a broad culture of skepticism and doubt. Harvard educator Howard Gardner is troubled by what he sees as a trend toward individual moral freedoms that could threaten the social fabric. Students are reluctant to judge the behavior of others as either ethical or unethical. He says,

> These students may not have read key texts by French and American intellectuals, but they have picked up some of their ways of thinking and expression. And so, over and over again, one hears that one person's truth may not be the same as another's; that two perspectives can be equally valid or equally right; that one has no right to judge people from another background or culture; that everyone has both good and bad properties.[5]

A survey of thirty thousand students in 2008 indicates that, in Gardner's words, "Young Americans seem to lack an ethical compass that governs their own behavior."[6]

David Brooks, political and cultural commentator for the *New York Times,* has this wonderfully insightful comment on morality in our time:

> For the past several centuries, most Westerners would have identified themselves fundamentally as Depraved Sinners. In this construct, sin is something you fight like a recurring cancer—part of a daily battle against evil. But these days, people are more likely to believe in their essential goodness. People who live by the Good Person Construct try to balance their virtuous self-image with their selfish desires. They try to manage the moral plusses and minuses and keep their overall record in positive territory. In this construct, moral life is more like dieting: I give myself permission to have a few cookies because I had salads for lunch and dinner. I give myself permission to cheat a little because, when I look at my overall life, I see that I'm still a good person. The Good Person isn't shooting for perfection any more than most dieters are following their diet 100 percent. It's enough to be workably suboptimal, a tolerant, harmless sinner and a generally good guy.[7]

Goodness is not under attack today, in the sense of a public distaste for goodness and a rush to what is evil. The idea of good is appreciated. Rather, there is genuine disagreement over what is good and whether there can be common agreement. Said another way, the notion of good is now fluid and dynamic, needing reassessment in new situations.

The Pebble in the Goodness Shoe

There may be many reasons why traditional notions of goodness are challenged today, but at root there is a pebble in the goodness shoe that makes walking difficult. This pebble is the idea of paired or binary opposites, like good/bad, right/wrong, just/unjust. There is nothing new in pairing such terms. In 1916, Ferdinand de Saussure claimed language is structured using opposites, thus *love* implies *hate, sick* implies *healthy,* and *hot* implies *cold.*[8] For language to have meaning, concepts must have complementary partners. However, there is something fresh in thinking that one cannot discuss one of these terms without the other being raised, most often unintentionally. Binary opposites are any set of terms taken to have opposite meanings. That is their nature: They cannot be separated and one raises the other. One affects how the other speaks, often undermining what is said. This pebble has made it necessary for preachers to alter their gait when talking about goodness. Because this pebble is not going away, it is important that we learn how to walk with it. If we do not realize that language has changed, we will persist in using it in ways that may not work effectively anymore. We may be like the person trying to communicate with a foreigner and who merely speaks louder. Something else is needed.

If we do not realize that language has changed, we will persist in using it in ways that may not work effectively anymore.

Saussure spoke about language. Jacques Derrida, Jean-François Lyotard, Linda Hutcheon, and other post-structuralists took his idea and applied it to social theory. The conversation spread beyond how words work to how some people use power in society. They used Saussure's idea of opposites to challenge the status quo. Western cultures tend to view binaries in hierarchical fashion. For instance, male/female is a binary. In culture, male was valued over female to the political advantage of men in power. Derrida argues that the privileging of one term that is "present" implies negating or marginalizing the other term that is "absent." Any individual speaker is likely to favor one term over another in a binary system, and this hierarchy is embedded within speech, betraying a speaker's biases and assumptions. These binaries can be identified and attacked in a process that has become widely known as deconstruction. A man might preach about the equality of men and women, yet tell stories only of men. His sermon might therefore be deconstructed as devaluing of women and making them invisible. Language works in that deconstructing way because binary oppositions and the hierarchies they represent are unstable; thus they can be toppled.

Preachers who are unaware how language works can fall into traps of their own making. To help counter the possibility of undermining one's own argument, one can use what we might call a goodness index. In sermon composition ask, *What binaries am I invoking that might speak to sensitive social issues?* Female/male may be obvious, but what about rich/poor—do I unintentionally privilege rich people over poor in my stories? Or with well/sick, do I presume that sickness is only the possession of those who do not appear well, or that people judged by others to be sick might not be more well than others in some ways? Or with disability/ability, do I presume to label some people as disabled and allow that to be the sum of their identity, in spite of many amazing abilities and gifts they possess?

Binary opposites are at the heart of the deconstructive process. By focusing on the marginalized or invisible term(s), one can deconstruct the power of the privileged term(s) and effect social change. In a novel, privileged rich people might be presented as good, but when that novel is examined for what it says about the poor, those same characters might start to appear in a different light.

In addition to binary opposites carrying hidden biases, a second problem with binary opposites is that they can imply only two choices, that a problem or situation is reducible to this or that, when in fact other possibilities exist. Preachers are particularly vulnerable to presenting false alternatives, partly because of the lingering modernist influence, and perhaps also because sermons must communicate a lot in a short time, so preachers take short cuts. We may say things like, "you must do this to be good" or "this is good and that is bad," as though there are no variables in between. When listeners raise questions about such use of binaries, the preacher's authority, power, and its legitimation are put in the spotlight. On the other hand, those who have been silenced may begin to find voice. Preachers can try to avoid either/or and instead look for positive ways to empower people, like other possible perspectives, circumstances, or stories that suggest a range of possibilities for faithful living, not just this or that.

We can never get rid of binary opposites. Even if we claim that the other pole is not present, the claim makes it visible. Opposites exist in what Derrida called a "trace" of memory that we might compare to an object's shadow. This "trace" makes meaning possible because it is always present and says "not this." As Derrida says, "The trace is in fact the absolute origin of sense in general."[9] He immediately adds, in his deconstructive manner, "Which amounts to saying once again that there is no absolute origin of sense in general."[10]

All of this might seem abstract and far removed from preaching, but the basic notions of deconstruction arose out of painful lived experience for Derrida. He grew up in Algeria in the 1930s when there was much local Islamic resistance to French colonists. As the child of French Jews he experienced racism and violence. Bigotry toward foreigners was accepted as "good." Deconstruction became an essential way for Derrida to survive. He began to subvert the common views. He believed that any single political position could become oppressive and the only escape was to keep meaning destabilized and in play. Closed systems of meaning are "totalizing" or totalitarian in suppressing counter examples. Unity is dangerous.

As a matter of interest, Derrida's problem with metaphysics and Christianity is that it tries to remove the "trace," to suppress countering polarities in the name of God.[11] Christianity represents for him a singularity, a totality, a "presence," a unity, a danger, and as one critic said on his behalf, it is "killing in the name of progress, mutilating on account of knowing the will of God better than others, etc."[12]

Still, Derrida said of himself that he was in "constant prayer." On the one hand, he said he was like a child who prays to a God who is like his own father, a strict, stern judge, but fair, and to a God who is also like his mother, always ready to declare him innocent (note the father/mother binary). On the other hand, he also prayed as an adult (note the child/adult binary), a philosopher asking critical questions like, to whom do you pray, for whom, and why?[13] He described both believer and nonbeliever (another binary) in himself as necessary because the person who is only a believer is not a believer. To believe one must also have serious doubts, be an atheist or at least be open to the possibility, otherwise faith is not faith.[14] For Derrida, the most one can do is to be open to the divine, and one does that best by subverting those powers that would reign.

Deconstruction and Theopoetry

Why should deconstruction matter for preachers? Derrida is not the Bible and most people in church haven't heard of him. Why not just dismiss these complex ideas as another language theory? The simple reason is that aspects of deconstruction have penetrated deep into our culture, even without people knowing where they came from.

As we have said, deconstruction is now understood to be part of how language works. Language is a human tool. Meaning is not singular. It is unstable and it tears itself apart. Single meanings are a power grab. Because meanings collapse, they must be constructed anew in each situation, not assumed to carry over from previous ones. Signs and words are no longer understood to communicate their meaning on their own. Red depends on other colors for its meaning (not this, or this...). There are no synonyms. Identities differ. Differences matter.[15] Because they are endless (not salmon red, not coral red, not...), all that we have are language games. Meaning is tentative, temporary, and illusory. One can never be confident of full understanding. Complete meaning is always deferred to some future time that never arrives.

Today's textbooks reflect these understandings, teachers teach them, media and technology communicate them, and friends demonstrate them. Derrida promoted and anticipated a mind-set pervasive in much Western culture.

Postmodernism is no organized movement and has no a master plan. A Christian girl in high school recently had her fifth friend commit suicide. Her mom asked her, "Have you ever thought of that?" "Well, yes." Startled, her mom asked, "So what keeps you from it?" "I won't because the kids need me at summer camp. It is just so hard to be different." Very little is trendy about believing in Jesus. Jesus as a person may be fine, Jesus dying on the cross is credible, Jesus as a great moral teacher is excellent, even Jesus as a prophet can be okay. But when we get to God becoming flesh in Jesus, or to Jesus rising from the dead, alive today, Christians can stand on very unappealing ground. Postmodern attitudes seem to attack any belief claims, and they offer very little to replace them.

Postmodernism is a parasite that chomps on the modern. It undermines dominant modernist ways of thought, like order, unity, and universal claims for truth. It knows no limits, however, and sometimes chomps on itself. It overthrows any attempt to stabilize meaning or to shield unexamined assumptions from criticism. It does not just attack modernist binaries. It can devour any thought. All in all, the seemingly pervasive nature of these critical attitudes could be enough to make a sensitive preacher feel paranoid, fearful of the pulpit, afraid of being dismissed, unable to utter a sound.

However, it is good for preachers to be aware that postmodernism can also be a theopoetic ally. Consider for example:

- Postmodern thought is open to differing perspectives, including Christian, while sophisticated critics in the modernist period sought to sideline the church. The church gets no preferential treatment, but religion has a rightful voice in the public sphere. To say something like, "I am a Christian because it brings out the poetry in life," might get a hearing.

- Postmodernism attacks order, unity, and stability, but it does so to prevent people from being excluded or silenced. In this regard, it takes seriously the command to love your neighbor as yourself.
- In the math of the modern period, order tended to mean conformity, and breaking out of established boxes of thought was a general no-no. Modernist math had difficulty with the 1 + 1 = 3 of story, as well as the 1 + 1 + 1 = 1 of the Trinity, but postmodern thought may be more open to such poetic truth.
- In being suspicious of absolute or totalizing claims, deconstruction may take the pervasive nature of sin and evil more seriously than many Christians. A mentor once taught, "We are most likely to sin when we are most sure we are right." David found that out when Nathan told him the parable in 2 Samuel 12. He was indignant that the rich man had stolen from the poor, until he realized he was the rich man.
- Derrida's call to overturn whatever powers reign in the moment seems to resonate with Jesus's frequent refrain to "repent" or turn around (*metanoia*)—repentance in theopoetic understanding is a continuing act, not just once for all time.
- Postmodernism is skeptical about knowledge. Those with vested interests determine what it is. This skepticism of knowledge finds support from Paul's thoughts on Christ, "It is written in scripture: *I will destroy the wisdom of the wise, and I will reject the intelligence of the intelligent*" (1 Cor 1:19; citing Isa 29:14).
- Postmodern caution not to assume certainty is anticipated by Paul's observation, "now we see through a glass, darkly" (1 Cor 13:12 KJV).

Theopoetry and Goodness

We speak in this chapter less about the nature of goodness than about the conditions needed to speak about goodness. Here are some positive suggestions concerning goodness and the pulpit. They are not just guidelines for preachers; they also are guidelines for our people, topics for discussion in sermons.

Be Invitational and Open to Other Meanings and Perspectives

If we say that a Bible text means only this, or that the cross means only one thing, we stop conversation with those for whom the meaning differs or is uncertain. Use phrases like: "from my perspective," "one way of thinking," "you may come at this differently." The same thing is true with controversial issues. Even if it seems like only one position is possible it does not make it so for others. There are always other perspectives. No one can claim a corner on truth. Meaning changes with context. Language is fragile. No matter how nuanced our expression, we cannot cement the meanings even of our own sermon. Misinterpretation is always possible—or perhaps nowadays misinterpretation does not exist, only differing interpretations, since intended meaning is not fully controlled. We cannot remove from our language deconstructive traces that contradict or undermine what we say. Of course preachers have always known that their own meanings are not the only ones that matter; there are meanings that the Holy Spirit intends.

Meaning changes with context.
Language is fragile.

We preach single-meaning address when we preach the faith as a closed system of thought. Listeners experience themselves either in or out, "do you believe it or not?" To avoid this as much as possible, solid teaching is needed that presents more than one way to view things. Still, bold speech or testimony is needed (heard as "this is what I believe"), but not as a means to close discussion (heard as "this is what you must believe"), and not as a continuous form of address in the sermon (heard as "what I say is all that matters"). Proclamation is also needed, first- to second-person address on behalf of God (heard as God saying, "I love you, I empower you, justice is mine"). The sermon can build toward it.[16]

Honor Differences

Related to the problem of single-meaning address is refusal to recognize differences. Even as words differ, opinions differ. Any difference is what Derrida called *différance,* a deliberately misspelled French word *(différence)* that employs a double entendre, *differ* and *defer* (an example of a word depending for meaning on a hypothetical endless string of other words).[17] In any congregation of believers, individuals differ in how they articulate faith. There is no end to differences. Even in churches where creeds are recited, not all people understand them the same way. Avoid (or be very careful using) generalizations like, "teenagers think," "women do this," "men love to . . .". Expectations of undue sameness can make some listeners feel invisible, unknown.

In spite of differences, realistically a preacher finally has to land somewhere and invite people to act in faithful ways. One cannot continually explore differences and defer meaning to another Sunday. Still, there is a way to speak of good actions so that they do not seem like closure, or finalized meaning. Invite people to act in humility, drawing on faith and the wisdom of the community, even if they cannot have absolute certainty about being right or avoiding sin.

Speak of Goodness in Relation to God

Goodness is not buttoned-down like math. Theopoetry questions, rethinks, and reimagines, allows for and honors other perspectives, traces clear paths of thought and image, and gives permission for listeners to have other perspectives. Preachers need not forfeit what they believe is good and true; they need only forfeit single-meaning address, uncritically repeating established modern formulas of long-established truth.

In speaking of good, use humility and be hospitable to others. The old preaching motto is "preach for something not against something." We cannot fully know what is good and we discern goodness best in dialogue and relationship to others. God's law, at least as we know and express it, does not cover all the variables of human experience. Laws offer standards, reliable indicators, and as George Lindbeck argued, grammar for good behavior.[18] Some preachers may insist that goodness is a divinely given system of abstract principles. Still, to invoke them as such has the effect on many people of shutting down conversation and foreclosing on their possible transformation.

Humility is also needed in relation to God. Goodness is best sought within a relationship with God and a community of faith. Goodness is not a system of abstract principles, and God is not static. We experience goodness because God continues to act in love toward all creation. In Genesis, no day was devoted to create goodness presumably because goodness resided first in God. Jesus said, "No one is good except the one God" (Luke 18:19). To know what is good is to know God, and we do this through prayer, scripture, worship, community, action, silence. Many ethicists tend to speak of goodness as though God is not involved, yet that distorts the reality many perceive in faith. When telling stories of someone good in a sermon, do not leave it there. Name God as the one who empowers that goodness. I cannot expect to be as good as a Mother Teresa, but I can expect to be good if I know that the same God who empowered her empowers me for my ministries. The problem with sermon determination of goodness according to law is that the person is portrayed as good or bad, when all people are a mixture of both, at least as I understand things. In determining goodness more on a case-by-case basis than on the basis of law, looking for goodness even in the midst of sin, there may be more opportunity to praise God, and more hope for the everyday person.

Scholars say that goodness and justice are social constructs. No doubt they are, but they may also be divine. Goodness and justice are necessary for societies to function; humans long for them when they are absent.[19] Still, goodness and ethical rules, like justice and the legal system, are not always to be equated. Some preachers might agree with Derrida that justice exists as a kind of trace or shadow of the legal system; we only glimpse it and do not have it in uncorrupted form. Notions of goodness and justice are necessarily deferred; they exist as a kind of promise that cannot be fully known.

Perhaps, as with beauty 1 and beauty 2, we need for our own purposes here to have two levels of goodness, goodness 1 being a world perspective and goodness 2 being goodness in relationship to God. Goodness 2 is not just the old fixed universal ideas of goodness; it is goodness as a loving ideal that we discern in glimpses and is illusive if we try to grasp it too tightly. Good is fluid, poetic, in motion. Goodness is God.

Use Deconstruction as a Source of Questions and New Perspectives

Encourage people to not rush to judgment concerning contemporary attitudes. They represent differing paradigms of thought influenced by the modern. Shyh-Jen Fuh of National Dong Hwa University in Taiwan says of deconstruction that it "is simultaneously ethical and non-ethical, exceeding incessantly the boundary of the ethical."[20] It treats knowledge of goodness as being always beyond our full grasp. "Thus we cannot say that deconstruction is ethically 'right' or 'wrong.' What it puts in question is precisely this conviction of and desire for a permanent truth."[21] Truth needs to be negotiated, thought through for the specific context.

The danger is that ethics can become totalizing, or as we might more commonly say, whatever is politically correct takes over everything. The comedy TV series *The Office* often found much humor in the totalizing methods of Michael, the boss. He would try to establish some new rule to improve office morale, like casual Fridays that others in the office thought he initiated in order to show off his "fun jeans" that he regularly had dry cleaned. Ethics can become "a new transcendental absolute, the ethic now so vehemently demanded testifies to a moralizing tendency that turns doxa into dogma: all discourses are obliged to dogmatically conform to the language of the ethical, that is, of a still-undefined ethics."[22]

Troy Jollimore in education has a vision of what ethics can be in this new age: "We might one day teach ourselves to stop looking at morality as an abstract and isolated set of requirements and demands—an external authority that stands apart from and sets limits on human existence—and see it instead as a set of commitments, enthusiasms, and passions that are woven into the very fabric of our lives."[23] Whether or not we agree with such proposals, they offer important alternatives that may ultimately help the church find even better ones in outreach to others.

Use Deconstruction to Assist Creativity

Deconstruction can assist sermon creativity. Every new liberation movement in the last half century has used deconstruction creatively as a way to empower those who have been silenced or marginalized. Deconstruction happens when terms are critically analyzed and found to contain contradictions. John McClure says that preaching insists on "the glory of the Infinite" and necessarily deconstructs reason, preventing it from contributing to human suffering.[24] Postcolonial criticism, third-wave feminism, race and ethnicity theory, gender studies, and so forth all use deconstruction as a means to undermine established authority, maintain discourse, mark differences, and avoid ultimate or fixed decisions. Derrida might not disagree with a play on words with *de construction* (= of construction) to refer to new meanings deconstruction positively generates. Deconstruction has a creative side in opening up possibilities not formerly seen, and in reducing the power of fixed systems that need change. One scholar says, "Derrida is useful both negatively, to facilitate an internal vigilance within Christian discourse . . . and positively . . . as the theological disrupts the secular, the immanent orders of the self-grounded."[25]

Avoid Singular Embrace of Deconstruction

At some point the postmodern denial of transcendence (i.e., no meaning comes from outside human language) itself becomes a totalizing claim. Phil Snider has done about as much as anyone might in adapting Derrida to the pulpit in his book, *Preaching after God.*[26] The danger in such a project is loss of much of the biblical story and language. Preachers who have followed that route have more often than not ended up articulating a faith that seems to negate much biblical witness and has little room for a God who acts, or for Jesus Christ. Just as logic cannot prove faith, reason and deconstruction cannot disprove it.

The modern era believed that God could be made to conform to tight categories of human reason. Derrida argued that that is what Christians have often done, but even he would avoid totalizing claims. He did not say "all Christians" do this or that the church "everywhere" does this "all of the time." Deconstruction gives essential understandings about language, but these too are fragmentary. Its conclusions need to be deconstructed in a never-ending process. Thus there is ample room for theopoetry, for the playfulness of its symbols, signs, metaphors, and images, for its manner of speech that invites participation and disagreement, and for the God it offers the world.

Chapter Five

Acts of Goodness (Homiletics)

Goodness has a beauty or poetry of its own. Although people commonly take good to be what is practical or effective, the poetry of goodness can best be seen in relation to God and God's purposes being made apparent. The poetry of goodness is roughly what Jesus referred to as the in-breaking of the kingdom or realm of God. We can think of goodness as glimpses of God or God's actions in creation and in human affairs and actions. Goodness is our acting as God would have us act. In this chapter we move to talk about practical and effective dimensions of goodness in homiletics. These homiletical guidelines are still within the larger frame of God's good actions on behalf of humanity; we are just concentrating on God's actions in and through the sermon. Goodness matters. Stories of goodness seen through the lens of the Bible change hearts, influence behavior, and shape communities. They are a means by which the goodness of God is known. Here we look at four key dimensions of homiletical practice that relate to goodness: good news, good grammar (the theological underpinnings of preaching), good form, and good acts (stories that might lead to action).

Good News

What is the good in *good news*? The gospel, as I understand it, is the saving action of God wherever found in the Old or New Testament. For Christians it is most plainly seen in the life, death, resurrection, ascension, and Second Coming of Jesus Christ. These different moments in the life and account of Jesus are theopoetic touchstones; each is open to interpretation, may be understood in different ways, is filled with mystery, and speaks to the wonder and beauty of God's caring love.

Whether the good news is communicated as actually good is a key issue for preaching. If those who need it most are turned off by the speaker, or by his or her attitudes, the gospel may have been uttered, but has it been received? Of course the Holy Spirit has a role. Whether people accept the news as good is not entirely up to preachers, and, as Frederick Beuchner once said referring to the way the gospel convicts its hearers, "The Gospel is bad news before it is good news."[1] Still, preachers play an important part in helping the gospel to be heard as good. In modernist thinking, the good news consisted of a good argument for what is good—ideas to be accepted and believed. Or, the good news was accompanied by an attack on the foolishness of those who believe otherwise, with messages akin to the Pharisee's self-congratulation, "God, I thank you that I'm not like everyone else—crooks, evildoers, adulterers—or even like this tax collector" (Luke 18:11).

In present times, the nature of language has radically affected how good news can be communicated. Craig Barnes has a good understanding of preaching as poetry. He says it is "revealing rather than arguing.... It doesn't argue, buttress against doubt, or defend. It explores. Then it unveils what it finds in voices such as awe, wonder, irony, or even anger and lament rather than instruction or debate. Poets are seldom accused of being convincing, but the best ones can transform the way we see life."[2] Language does not only communicate information, it generates experience, it creates events, it performs actions. Authors no longer control their own meaning. Language is unstable, assumptions must be reexamined, meaning is illusive and fragmentary. Good news will not be accepted as good simply because a preacher declares it to be. And resistance to such declaration is not necessarily indicative of the hard hearts of listeners.

For good news to be heard as good, preachers need poetry. They also need to be intentional in naming what opposes it. For example, a fifth grade boy was sent to the principal's office for repeatedly addressing his teacher by her first name. If a preacher said that the good news is that he can be taught not to be rude, it reduces the gospel to having nice manners. More than this, notions of both bad and good need to be open for reexamination. If the boy is continually rude, the problem may lie in his home life, and the gospel needs to be heard to address the roots of the problem.

> For good news to be heard as good, preachers need poetry.

Bad is also not just "others" and good is not just "us." Bad and good reside in all. Preachers can earn the trust of contemporary listeners by beginning to deconstruct the very message they the preachers construct, indicating other contrasting possibilities or interpretations.

Problematizing Sermons

Words live and die in sound. They also die and live when deconstructive processes are engaged. Even language must die and be born again. Preachers can assist deconstruction within the sermon by critiquing common assumptions and attitudes, or expressing opposing viewpoints, or exposing possible contradictions in one's own thought. When preachers resist deconstruction, their messages may become more rigid and in danger of collapse, like a building that is not designed to bend in hurricane winds.

Sermons need to be problematized. Competing claims need to be voiced and legitimate questions and perspectives raised and honored. A simple way to problematize a sermon is during sermon preparation. Ask simple questions of the theme sentence, like the following:

- What claim is made about God?
- What do I find beautiful and good about this claim?
- What do I find unsettling?
- What emotions does it raise and why?
- Who might be affirmed or empowered by God's action?
- Who might feel threatened?
- Who might feel excluded?
- What is the best reason to accept this claim?
- What is the best reason to reject it?

- On what basis do I say what I say?
- What are my unexamined assumptions?
- What other perspective might someone legitimately hold?

Only one or two of these questions might appear in the sermon itself. For example, in relation to John 9, the theme sentence might be: "Jesus heals the man born blind." It is a beautiful story. Since economy of sermon time is key, the deconstruction impulse is best used where it matters most, in relation to the theme sentence. In spite of its beauty, the sentence shouts an unsettling question, *What about those who are born blind who are not given their vision?* (In fact, that is a version of the question asked by the disciples, "Rabbi, who sinned so that he was born blind, this man or his parents?" [John 9:2].) Rather than suppress the tough questions that might threaten to deconstruct the entire sermon if voiced, we as preachers should openly acknowledge them and pursue them. But in doing so we also need to do our theological or theopoetic homework and offer a reading of the text to set alongside the protest. As the closing dialogue of John's story makes readily apparent (9:35-41), the real sight the man receives is seeing Jesus as his Lord. As Jesus says, "I have come into the world...so that those who don't see can see" (John 9:39), and there are some in the world who see and who are blind.

Creating Tension in Sermons

Theopoetic preaching also needs texture and tension that deconstruction can help supply. Something has to be at stake, something has to happen, there needs to be plot and action, the sermon needs to matter. It has to meet the felt need of people, perhaps a longing for justice, or a hunger for peace, or a need for forgiveness. An old saw goes, a sermon should have something for the head, something for the heart, and something for the hands.

A recent sermon on prayer had good teaching. The preacher provided examples of prayer from the Bible and spoke about the value of prayer in our lives. But the sermon had as much appeal as a dish of ice cream outdoors in a blizzard. The preacher did not deconstruct prayer. The preacher would have got our rapt attention by speaking about prayers that seem to go unanswered. The sermon would then have movement, purpose, bite, drive, and suspense: How will the preacher account for unanswered prayers? Are prayers just for our own benefit? Did Jesus not really mean, "Ask, and you will receive. Search, and you will find. Knock, and the door will be opened to you" (Matt 7:7)? Can it be that all prayers are answered? Again, 1 + 1 = 3. Some twist, some tension is needed.

The preacher ought not ask too many questions and should not be heard to have all the answers. Preachers can ask questions that have no completely adequate answer, like, why is there evil? Or the preacher can express ideas that counter the theme sentence, like God often seems not to hear our prayers. Such strategies open gaps in the sermon, spaces for mystery and wonder. If a sermon seems too simple, too easy, too buttoned down, there is no room for listeners to participate, and there is little interest for them. By problematizing or deconstructing the ideas in the theme sentence, the sermon as a whole is problematized; it gains conflict, texture, and interest.

If a sermon seems too simple, too easy, too buttoned down, there is no room for listeners to participate.

Modern preaching tended to make everyone be of one mind, and in doing so often rendered the congregation mute before the superior knowledge of the preacher. Rather, preaching should render the congregation articulate, "speaking the truth with love" (Eph 4:15), able to speak, even about differences, without fear of division. Jesus said, "that they may all be one" (John 17:21 NRSV), but there is more than one way his words may be understood. Hans Urs von Balthasar makes a valuable distinction between modern notions of unity and more fulsome symphonic or Christian notions rooted in God: "People cannot bear to have unity that is above them and of which . . . they are only part. They shift unity from the whole into the part. They do not want symphony, but rather unison. In Platonic terms this is the *tyrannis*; in modern terms it is totalitarianism."[3] Unity today is perhaps best achieved not through conformity and sameness but through reliance upon the Holy Spirit to form communities of love that welcome difference, symphonies with many parts and players.

Using Polar Energy in Sermons

No two opposing notions are more important for preaching or for theology in general than trouble and grace, also known as law and gospel, crucifixion and resurrection, judgment and grace, sin and forgiveness, brokenness and healing, anthropocentric and theocentric, bad news and good news, what we do and what God does, homelessness and homecoming, and the like. To these pairs I add one more set: math (how the world often operates) and poetry (how God operates). These paired terms do not all mean exactly the same thing and their differences matter, but they are all closely related. If there were just one set of terms that could fully capture the range of meanings here, and the importance of this polarity, we would use it. All together they communicate a powerful source of potential polar energy for the sermon. Whenever we hear theology at its best, some dynamic of these poles is responsible. Whenever a sermon gets to God in a powerful way, these poles are present for this simple reason: Speaking about trouble without preaching grace mostly leaves God out, and preaching grace with no relationship to trouble offers a smarmy God. Both poles, trouble and grace, are true though they are opposing. Without polar energy, a sermon may sound boring, irrelevant, or totalizing.

Saussure observed that meaning is generated in the interplay between opposites like bad and good, hot and cold. Paul knew it when he wrote to the Romans about law and gospel, as did Augustine when he claimed these terms as essential keys to interpret the Bible. Perhaps the pair of terms with the broadest range is trouble and grace. Trouble is how things are so often in life, messed up and complicated. Trouble is sin, brokenness, despair, heartache, illness, evil, injustice and so on. It is also what God requires us to do by way of law. Law is a gift but we fail if we try to do it all on our own. We are like Paul in this regard, "I can will what is right but I cannot do it. For I do not do the good I want, but the evil I do not want is what I do" (Rom 7:18-19 NRSV). If that is true for Paul, it must be for us as well. Denominations have argued over whether humans are capable of doing good on their own, but regardless, God is the author of all good, or as James says, "Every good gift, every perfect gift, comes from above" (1:17), or as Jesus said, "Without me you can't do anything" (John 15:5).

Grace, by contrast, is God's action. It is what God does to empower or save us, through no merit of our own. The dynamic of trouble and grace makes theopoetic meaning possible. Sermons rightly harness the tension between the poles by moving from one to the other. They may be poles that keep reappearing, or they may govern the deep grammar of the entire sermon. I suggest that the sermon follow the overall plot of faith and move from trouble to grace, from the Exodus to the promised land, from Good Friday to Easter, from the fall in Eden to the New Jerusalem. Let the first half of the sermon be trouble and the second half grace. There is movement in the other direction in the Bible, but that is the direction of sin and evil.

Good news moves overall from Good Friday to Easter, not from resurrection to crucifixion or from the New Jerusalem to the fall. Theopoetic sermons need movement and plot. Moreover they need roughly equal emphasis on trouble and grace in the shorter sermons of today. In this manner they may speak not only to the need for God's action but also introduce listeners to God and "equip the saints for the work of ministry" (Eph 4:12 NRSV).

Trouble and grace (or whatever similar terms we use) need to be understood and applied in dynamic ways. They are not to be used in modern mechanical or mathematical ways, like 1 + 1 = 2. They generate tension because they seem contradictory and are more like 1 + 1 = 3. By being harnessed and placed in relationship, they make new meaning. Modernist thought never quite appreciated the electricity that flows between these poles. It misconceived trouble to grace as problem to solution, failing to recognize that law is not just a problem and grace is not about solutions; grace is about a relationship with God in which solutions may certainly come, but faith is the goal, not solving just one problem. Or, trouble was conceived to be simply a foil. Once grace is reached, trouble is cancelled out in what rhetoric used to call a straw argument. Not so; the trouble and the grace are both real and true, in good postmodern contradictory fashion. In the tension between trouble and grace we "work out [our] own salvation in fear and trembling" (Phil 2:12 NRSV).

Luther kept such terms alongside each together always interacting, for example, in his notion of a Christian as *simil justus et peccator* (at the same time both saved and sinner.) Late in his life Derrida said that he thought Christianity was particularly well equipped for self-criticism and ongoing renewal of the sort he envisioned deconstruction might enable.[4] It may well have been this tension of trouble and grace that he sensed. In the dynamic of trouble and grace, deconstruction is built-in and ongoing, as is construction of new meaning. Still, in the theopoetic sermon as I conceive it, grace is stronger because, as in the Bible, it has the final word. Grace is, after all, the word of life.

It is a puzzle to me why even many teachers of homiletics tend to be silent in their publications on what constitutes the good news and how best to communicate it, given both its vitality for preaching and the nature of academic inquiry to engage discussion. I know one excellent preacher who denies trouble and grace yet perhaps unconsciously uses the dynamic all the time in his sermons. Sermons often succeed or fail on the basis of whether they get to God, whether the gospel is preached in theopoetic ways. Joanna Adams says that the purpose of preaching "is to help people see the events in their lives and in human history from God's point of view."[5] Cleophus

J. LaRue says in African American traditions people worship, "to be assured and reassured that God has acted and will act for them and for their salvation."[6] Eugene Peterson says, "Preaching announces what God is doing right here and now, at this time and in this place.... Preaching is language that involves us personally with God's actions in the present."[7] My own perspective is related: If preaching is to introduce people to God and not just ideas about God, then the sermon in some way needs to arrive at God's saving actions.[8] That is why the theme sentence focusing on what God is doing in or behind the text is so utterly crucial. If sermons are silent on God in the sermon, exactly how will God be known as a player in people's lives? If sermons are silent on God, how do they differ from a Toastmasters talk?

Good Grammar

This is not primarily a discussion about sermon form: Trouble and grace are an essential theological dynamic in nearly any form of sermon. This discussion is about theological grammar, deep structure functioning beneath the surface like linguistic grammar rules. In one way of thinking, there seem to be rather limited options for the preacher: If not the gospel, then what? If not God, then why? If not by trouble and grace, then how? There may be other perspectives to take, but in my experience, every sermon has either trouble or grace, most have trouble, and the best have both.

Even some experienced preachers resist a theme sentence; they preach on a general topic like love and they risk lack of focus. Maybe they assume the congregation should be able to figure out what the sermon says. Other preachers resist focusing a theme sentence on God's action in the biblical text and they focus instead on what people must do. They risk bypassing God. They may assume the congregation knows about God, who in any case does not need to be in every sermon. Still other preachers focus on God but resist focusing on an action that sounds like good news, so they focus on God's demands. Perhaps they assume the congregation will do good on their own in spite of sin and evil. They may inadvertently condemn the congregation to no help from God.

Practical Step 1: Reading Texts by Inversion

Many preachers do not follow trouble and grace because they have not heard of them homiletically, or they do not think that both are present in every text. Some biblical scholars who may have unknowingly detached themselves from the need for preachers to preach the gospel, think that it unfairly imposes on the biblical text a theological template—as though Paul and most preachers throughout the ages did not do this as an intentional exercise in reading scripture in the light of Christ and his message of new life. Here is an exercise to help preachers find trouble and grace in nearly any biblical passage. Once trouble and grace are located in the text, the preacher will then be able to quickly sketch the sermon, so this is a very useful exercise to engage in, especially early in the week.

Derrida said that an opposite pole exists as a "trace" or faint image, even when it is not articulated. The same thing is true in reading biblical texts for trouble and grace. If trouble is not apparent, one can read a text by a process of inversion to find it. Or, if grace is not apparent, read it by inversion to find the trouble. Trouble and grace are both implied, but they may not be fully evident in the preacher's mind. Think of inversion as finding the mirror image of a text, and then test it to be sure that it is in fact a fair reading of it. This can be a playful exercise that heightens creative options for a preacher. It can be quickly illustrated using ideas of trouble and grace drawn from Luke 13:31-35:[9]

START WITH	INVERSION TO
Trouble	*Grace:*
Herod seeks to kill Jesus.	Jesus seeks to save Herod.
Jerusalem will kill Jesus.	Jesus will die for Jerusalem.
Jerusalem will not see Jesus until they know him.	Jesus will be present but unrecognized.
Grace	*Trouble*
Jesus casts out demons.	Demons would cast out Christ.
Jesus will finish his work.	Humans cannot finish what is required of them.
Jesus would be as a mother hen.	We do not choose nurture.
Jerusalem will name Jesus Blessed.	Without Christ we may feel cursed.

One could do the same exercise using ideas of trouble and grace from our world:

START WITH	INVERSION TO
Trouble	*Grace:*
We must trust God.	God gives us trust.
We must help others.	God works through us.
Do what God instructs.	God empowers us.

Try this exercise early in the week with your sermon. Begin with the theme sentence that identifies an action of God (grace) and see what the inverse of it is, that is, why God acted in that way. What was the trouble? Or if you cannot find grace in your text, invert the trouble to find it. Trouble and grace are grammatical elements of theology in any age. They mirror each other.

Here are the simplest helpful definitions of trouble and grace. *Trouble puts the burden on people to do something.* So if it feels like a weight, it probably is trouble. *Grace puts the burden on God, and God in Christ has accepted it.* So if it feels like a good gift, it probably is grace. You can use this simple test to help you distinguish between them if ever you are in doubt.

Practical Step 2: Structuring the Grammatical Underpinnings of a Sermon

Inversion can be immensely useful to determine the theological underpinnings of a sermon you compose. In Isaiah 52:13-53:12, the Suffering Servant, if the theme sentence is "God raised up the Suffering Servant," the inverse trouble that leads to it can be "The servant suffered" or "God seemed absent." That gives the overall movement of the sermon, from one to the other: the trouble arises from what the text says about "The servant suffered." The grace of the second half of the sermon arises from this mirroring textual idea "God raised up the Suffering Servant."

If you preached that sermon right now you would be stuck in the biblical text, you would not speak about present day. One more essential ingredient is needed. Transpose each of those sentences from then to now, by changing one or two words. Thus we end up with four sentences to guide the sermon movement. It is more easily demonstrated than explained:

(1) Trouble in the biblical text: The servant suffered.

(2) Trouble in our world: Many today suffer.

(3) Grace in the biblical text: God raised up the Suffering Servant.

(4) Grace in our world: God blesses our ministry of sacrifice.

These four sentences guide what I call the four pages (or quarters) of a sermon.[10]

Here is the same process again: Start with a theme sentence. One about the Prodigal Son might be "The father welcomes home his lost son." Look for the flip side of the grace, and the trouble is "The son was lost." Putting them in trouble-to-grace order, and transposing each from then to now, we get:

(1) Trouble in the biblical text: The son was lost.

(2) Trouble in our world: Many are lost.

(3) Grace in the biblical text: The father welcomes home his lost son.

(4) Grace in our world: God welcomes home the lost.

Let's try one more example, using 1 Corinthians 2:1-5. This is a difficult text in part because Paul's action seems more in focus than God's. The emphasis is anthropocentric, and if you preached what Paul did in coming to Corinth, you would probably end up just telling us what we have to do, and you would not proclaim the gospel. However, if one looks more closely using inversion to find God's mirroring action of grace and empowerment, that action becomes apparent:

> When I came to you, brothers and sisters, I didn't come preaching God's secrets to you like I was an expert in speech or wisdom. I had made up my mind not to think about anything while I was with you except Jesus Christ, and to preach him as crucified. I stood in front of you with weakness, fear, and a lot of shaking. My message and my preaching weren't presented with convincing wise words but with a demonstration of the Spirit and of power. I did this so that your faith might not depend on the wisdom of people but on the power of God. (1 Cor 2:1-5)

Again, start sermon preparation by determining the theme sentence and then work by inversion to find an appropriate trouble focus.

(1) Trouble in the biblical text: Paul felt foolish preaching.

(2) Trouble in our world: We may feel foolish testifying.

(3) Grace in the biblical text: God empowers Paul preaching the cross.

(4) Grace in our world: God empowers our ministries.

This simple four-sentence exercise can save hours of sermon preparation time by providing early in the week the bare bones of a sermon that gets to good news. The time saved can be devoted to imaginatively enlivening each of the four pages and the overall flow. To flesh out the pages, simply interact with each sentence, one at a time. For instance with 1 Corinthians 2:1-5, above, write a quarter of the length of your sermon establishing from the biblical text that Paul felt foolish in preaching (page one). Then switch to our time as speak of the difficulties we have in sharing our faith (page two). At the half-way point, switch to show that God empowers Paul preaching the cross (page three), and then move to God empowering our ministries (page four). Such structure assists theopoetry. Because as a preacher you don't have to spend the whole week wandering in the Sinai looking for direction, you can pay immediate attention to crafting a message that gets to God and addresses head, body, and heart. We might say in summary that most sermons today need an MRI: Movement to grace, Relationship with God, and Imagination serving God.

Now try giving an MRI to your own sermon in progress.

Practical Step 3: Intertextual Practice

Derrida and others describe how any speech is a text that pulls in other texts. This deliberate use of one text to shape the meaning of another is called intertextuality. This is a particularly postmodern way of reading: Texts, like words, gain meaning in relation to other texts or words. The New Testament writers commonly use texts from the Old Testament and place them alongside the events in the life, ministry, and teachings of Jesus.

In late modern practice, preachers took a Bible passage and read it in relation to the verses around it and the literary purposes of the biblical author. They assumed the adequacy of that act to communicate the gospel, or that people already sufficiently understood the gospel. God was rarely a sermon focus, much less an empowering or saving action of God. The modern focus tended to be on what we have to do, what we should do in light of Christ's sacrifice for us. We now understand that relatively few texts on their own, lifted out of their context in the Bible as a whole, speak about the central events at the heart of Christian faith: the incarnation and Jesus life, the cross and resurrection, the ascension, and the Second Coming. Arguably, all of the New Testament books depend on these various connections, they presume them, and they are an important part of how texts are to be read. The gospels were not composed of individual stories that are to be read separate from the cross and resurrection, or independent of the true identity of Jesus Christ. Christian texts depend on intertextual reading. The postmodern age revels in intertexual readings of all sorts. In the simplest expression of intertextual practice for preaching, one that can and perhaps should be used in every sermon, preachers can look for some kind of echo with the Christ event to help reinforce and amplify the gospel content of their particular biblical text.

The reason this type of intertextual reading is so vital is this: Most people in church don't know their Bibles, and some fail to own one. Christian faith is rooted in Jesus Christ, his life, teachings, death, resurrection, ascension, and final return. Together these events and the various perspectives we have on them form the gospel at the heart of our faith. Most texts on their own do not speak of this larger picture. If a sermon is based on John 9, and the gospel story is not mentioned, on what basis are the people to believe that Jesus healed the blind man? On the authority of the preacher? Or of this one passage of scripture? Or of the church? For some good-hearted people that might be enough, but in an age of skepticism, why should people believe something if it is in no way a part of their experience? However, if the healing of the blind man is linked to Jesus's resurrection from the dead, the listeners are at least allowed an appeal to their own experience. Is Jesus alive or not? Does he have that power, and if so, would I deny his power to give sight and faith? Has this not already happened to me in my receiving faith?

This linking to the gospel is one of the most important yet underpracticed forms of intertexuality for preachers and it is so necessary in the postmodern age. It brings key points in the Christ event alongside the preached text and it relies on these key events to communicate the identity of Jesus, at least as witnessed by the biblical authors. To my mind it could be part of any sermon because it brings the congregation into a face-to-face encounter with the living God.

To take another example, if one brings the Prodigal Son alongside the incarnation, Jesus can be seen as one who in becoming human went to a far country on our behalf to get us by entering our death, rising from the dead, and returning to the loving Father. Such echoes do more than provide poetic resonance: They invite yet another layer of meaning in relation to a text. Because this latter echo is the very stuff of the gospel, it brings the gospel into focus in a way that individual texts typically fail to do.

Alternatively, bring this parable alongside the cross, from which Jesus in effect says the same words to us that the father says to his prodigal son: "You were dead and have come back to life! You were lost and are found!" It is one thing to overhear a father say those words to a son; it is even more intimate to be reminded that Jesus says those words to all Christians in their baptism and to all who seek him. Yet another preaching alternative is to hear God say those same joyous words to Jesus and us at Easter—we tend to overlook God's joy.

Intertextual Exercise: Connecting to the Larger Story

To help preachers connect their own preaching text with the larger Christian story, here are a few questions they may ask of their text:

(a) Ask, how may God's saving action in or behind the biblical text be seen to resonate with God's action in coming in Jesus Christ, or in raising Jesus from the dead, or in Jesus sending his Spirit and sitting at the right hand of God, or fulfilling all divine promises at the end of time in the Second Coming? The issue here may not be whether a preacher is a literalist or not, the issue is whether the preacher will allow the poetry of the Bible to speak in its powerful richness and plurality of meanings.

(b) Ask, does the resurrection affect the meaning of even Jesus's words? For example, in Matthew 25:31-46, Jesus speaks about the end of time and how the Son of Man will divide all of the nations into the sheep and the goats. That text is a terrifying text, for who has not passed by a beggar, a hospital, or prison and thereby failed to care for Jesus? By the literal terms of the text we are all goats—and it is important we know it and do better.

That truth needs to stand. Over and against it, however, is this: If all of the nations are divided into sheep and goats, the teams are not going to be even. There will be a multitude of goats on the goat side and over on the sheep side there will be one lone sheep, only one who is innocent, the Lamb of God.

As a goat, I figure that Jesus already knew the composition of the teams when he told this parable. No sooner does Jesus finish telling it than he turns to his disciples and announces that the Son of Man will be crucified within the week (Matt 26:1-2). That is fascinating. In other words, he is not just going to the cross to die, he is going to die for the goats. As Jesus says earlier in Matthew to the Pharisees, "Those who are well have no need of a physician, but those who are sick. Go and learn what this means, 'I desire mercy, not sacrifice.' For I have come to call not the righteous but sinners" (9:12-13 NRSV). Jesus came to save the sinners. He died for the goats. He died to save the goats. He rose again to sit at the right hand of God on behalf of the goats. He is God's judge. He is God's judgment. He is God's payment for our sins. He is the one who pays for us when we come up short at the final checkout counter. He comes over to us as we vainly pat our pockets and purge our purses looking for the means to pay, and he says, "I see you are a goat. Goat, I love you. I love *you*. Let me pay for *you*. I desire mercy, not sacrifice. Won't you let me offer you my cloak that you might share in my innocence and glory?" And to all of us who want to follow in his way he drapes over our shoulders his sheep's cloak that we might not only look like sheep but also be counted as sheep by our God. In our baptism we become goats in sheep's clothing. The Lamb of God: 100 percent pure Lamb's wool.[11]

(c) Ask what other biblical texts speak to the text or topic at hand, either supporting or seeming to contradict it? Often these can be found with a word search on the Internet. With the sheep and the goats, above, it was helpful that the other texts cited by Matthew (i.e., about the crucifixion of the Son of Man and Jesus coming to save sinners not those who are well) are from the same book of the Bible. One need not be limited in this way, however: Matthew is the lone gospel that makes no mention of Jesus as the Passover Lamb or Lamb of God (an example of reading the cross through the textual lens of the Passover).

(d) Ask, is there some way in which the action of a biblical character in some way anticipates or echoes the actions of Jesus Christ? For instance, Adam is the first human and Jesus is the first person of the New Creation; Adam's sin became the death of all, where Jesus's death became the life of all. Or, Moses led his people out of bondage to the promised land, as does Jesus. Moses strikes the rock and water comes forth to save the people, and Jesus is the living water who saves. Or, Esther saves her people when the odds seem impossible and Jesus does the same. The biblical writers often employ such echoes or types to serve the gospel, and current preachers can do the same. The type, through poetry, points to Christ.

(e) Ask, if someone came to church for the first time, would he or she get a sense from this sermon of the heart of Christian faith? If not, is there some bridge to the larger gospel story that can lead them poetically to the bigger picture? Perhaps a preacher has painted a picture of how bad things are; the preacher can always take that same situation and imagine for the congregation what it looks like when God's love is allowed to flow uninterrupted.

In summary, how we might use what these questions reveal? Few biblical texts, including the New Testament, actually contain the gospel: The gospel is the larger message, the good news in Christ and its consequences in society today. By practicing intertextual linking between one's text and the larger story, a preacher strengthens not only the good news but also the sense of empowerment people in the pews receive. Preachers unfamiliar with this practice might start simply, first by making links to the cross and resurrection, and then gradually experimenting with other key aspects of Jesus's story that give witness to his identity. In practical terms, intertexual linking is a fairly late stage of sermon preparation and it normally might appear late in the sermon, once the good news from one's own preaching text is fully established and honored.

Good Form

Sermons need some kind of form and structure; they cannot be just blobs of sound. In the modern era, sermon form was largely superficial and was disconnected from sermon content. A sermon form was chosen and, like a mold, it was filled with discursive ideas. Sermons were to address the mind. They might be doctrinal, exploring a doctrine; topical, probing a social issue; expository or exegetical, explaining what a text said and meant; or special occasion, as for a funeral or Memorial Day or Remembrance Day. They might be point form or free flowing, university sermons (academic) or parish, for adults or for children.

Within the last fifty years, narrative sermons have begun to meet postmodern demands for less emphasis on reason and logic as the only ways to learn. Even here there are varieties, entire narratives based either in biblical time or our own, episodic sermons using narrative intermittently, sermons that move by plot, sermons that develop a single image, sermons influenced by the shape and function of the biblical text, and so forth.

Postmodern sermon forms, like postmodern art, tend to be eclectic or hybrid. Exterior structure does not necessarily rule; deeper kinds of structure are also possible, for instance, based in different kinds of theology and social perspectives, or in the Four Pages as deep grammar. We cannot yet be sure what forms will emerge but two related possibilities are bricolage and rhizomatic.

Bricolage Structure

"Trouble to grace" can be a sermon form in itself, but it is a grammar first and foremost, and can be consciously employed in most current sermon forms to enhance theopoetic potential. Postmodern art gives preachers some new ways to think about sermon form. *Bricolage* is from the French word for puttering or tinkering, and it is used these days to describe the making of things from a range of materials at hand, like creating music from found objects like hubcaps, bottles, pots, and pans. In 1962, French anthropologist Claude Lévi-Strauss used the term *bricolage* to describe how in some societies practical creative problem solving focuses on reusing available materials. This was in contrast to the creativity of an engineer who has a goal of crossing a river and determines the mechanical means to do so using math.[12]

Preachers are local theologians who craft sermons as bricolage from the materials of life around them: stories from books and conversations, images from daily life, ideas from Bible commentaries, teachings from history, and items from news and entertainment. Many preachers have conceived sermons in this manner for some time without knowing the term. Perhaps the most common example of this is sermons designed around the use of visual or audio media; pictures or music at some point in the sermon; or moving into song, as African American celebration has done for generations, and as Luke Powery has recently explored using spirituals in part as a form of celebration.[13]

Rhizomatic Structure

Another good way to think of theopoetic sermons is in relation to rhizomes. A rhizome is a species of grass that grows sideways without a center, each node sending out roots and shoots. If cut in one place it grows in another. It has many chains or links.[14]

Rhizomatic structure does not follow a strict linear line of thought as in the manner of a point form of address, where the appeal is to reason and the points add up to an argument designed to persuade. Points work vertically, aiming toward a definite goal. A rhizomatic sermon, by contrast, moves horizontally in a network pattern. Various elements, characteristic of bricolage, offer different kinds of appeal: reason, emotion, the senses, kinesthetic, intuitive, and so on. Stories, quotations, images, biblical sections, news items, and so on are arranged in a manner that sometimes leads logically and sometimes by association or image. Rhizomatic sermons do not try to persuade through argument so much as to influence by presenting a perspective or persepectives. Many preachers already structure their sermons in this manner. Essentially it is a looser structure than one that works by math: this plus this plus this equals this. It still must hold together, it must have coherence, people must be able to understand what is happening, it cannot be just a jumble of things. Clarity allows for listener participation. Each sermon is made of fragments, each of which has inherent interest and the hearer is involved at each stage, awaiting to see how it will all come together. Any one sermon is never the whole story, but is a part of an ongoing event that can never be fully captured.

The theme sentence is of particular importance in such a sermon because it is what the sermon is about. If lost, the sermon self-destructs. Thus the sermon should never go far from it. Ideas cluster around it. A link to it is what all the fragments have in common.

The sermon should never go far from the theme sentence.

I preached to a group of clergy a sermon on Isaiah 52:13–53:12, the Suffering Servant. A list of my paragraphs will indicate what rhizomatic structure looks like, though such a summary of course removes poetry. (1) People lack interest in history. They don't care that "God blessed the suffering of the servant and raised him high above all others." (This was the theme sentence.) (2) Preachers have to make things contemporary. Story: Natalie Cole recorded a duet of "Unforgettable" using the original rendition by her father, Nat King Cole. Our text is a duet, a love song to the Suffering Servant (with quotations from it). (3) People still may not care about Isaiah. A preacher might need to speak to some real need the people feel, like why does God cause suffering? That's what Israel believed about the Servant, that God caused his suffering. That might catch interest. (4) Story of a recent auction in Nebraska of five hundred cars that had been bought new since the 1950s and had been stored in a field, not driven. (5) Some of our suffering churches are on the auction block. (6) Why does a good God allow suffering (of the church and of people)? (7) Sometimes stories are the best response, like God correcting the people in our text. God did not cause the Servant's suffering but blessed him and lifted him up (theme sentence). (8) Story: a minister in sacrificial ministry forgot that God was in control, not him. (9) Story: a church involved in sacrificial ministry relied on the Holy Spirit when things did not make sense. (10) Story: a man in sacrificial ministry found himself in the presence of Christ. (11) Theme sentence and hope: that people would be similarly blessed in their own ministries of sacrifice.

Most important, in this sermon I did not try to answer how a good God can allow suffering. It simply surfaced as a key question. Theopoetic preachers need to decide not only what they will say about God but also what they will leave unsaid, as mystery. One can best decide by knowing one's people well.

Of course there are many other possible designs for theopoetic preaching. Traditional forms can be used, and Ronald J. Allen gives a fresh summary of these in his recent *Sermon Treks: Trailways to Creative Preaching* (Nashville: Abingdon Press, 2013). He includes preaching in relation to calendar events, lectionary and non-lectionary preaching, topical preaching, preaching on social issues, series preaching, doctrinal preaching, and so forth.

Presentation guru Nancy Duarte suggests that the structure of great talks is a comparison between what is and what could be. She demonstrates using Steve Jobs's 2007 speech launching the iPhone as well as the "I Have a Dream" speech of Dr. Martin Luther King Jr. The beginning of the speech talks about what is and she diagrammatically represents that on a chart as a horizontal line. Then a vertical line jumps at right angles up to a new higher horizontal level as King creates as much of a gap as possible between what is and what could be. The line moves horizontally for a little and then drops back down to the original horizontal plain as King speaks about what is. By the end of the speech the diagram looks like several buildings of similar height rising from a flat horizon. The speech ends on the high level, with a rousing endorsement of what could be.[15]

Yet another option for theopoetic structure is suggested by Craig Barnes. Perhaps inspired by Schleiermacher's notion of interpretation as a hermeneutical circle or spiral, or perhaps by Eugene Lowry's notion of the sermon as a loop, Barnes says this:

> Poets don't make arguments; they reveal mysteries. This doesn't mean that minor poets can't state claims in their sermons, but they don't follow a strict linear path of logic. They don't worry about logic at all. Instead, they explore the sacred mystery they are attempting to unveil to the congregation. And this typically means that their points follow the path of a spiral. The sermon is not a circle, since it does make progress, but as with all interesting explorations, it doesn't move in a straight line.[16]

Good Actions

Good stories do more than catch our attention; they introduce us to good people and remind listeners of goodness in others. For example, William often looked in on a ninety-eight-year-old woman who lived alone and still shoveled her own walk in winter. After a bad ice storm the power lines were down and he was leaving town. A lawyer lived across the street who most folks thought to be gruff and standoffish. No one else being around, William asked him if he could look in on the woman. Even before William had departed he spotted out the window the lawyer crossing the road with a pot of tea and a steaming bowl of soup.

Good stories also introduce us to people who are vulnerable and in need. A woman contemplating suicide is drawn into a noon hour concert in a church and finds herself reaching for a pew Bible; a man attends the graduation of his child and suddenly realizes he doesn't know any of his offspring; an insecure girl comes home with a first prize for her watercolor paintings. These are poignant moments in life, and in precisely such moments one may look for some sign of God, startling and unexpected, like a flower poking through spring snow. But then in my understanding, there is no time in which one cannot look for a sign from God and expect to find it.

Good preaching has an outcome in the lives of listeners. What does this mean in an age where "knowledge, reason, and morality do not reside within the mind of the individual, but within relationships,"[17] and where knowledge is "the result of active interchange between people in reciprocal relationships"?[18] Morality has undergone a change, but preachers may still find traction if they can change as well, if they can allow perspectives (including other than those of the church) to be heard respectfully.

Good preaching has an outcome in the lives of listeners.

Contemporary values and attitudes towards moral and ethical goodness of many people today resemble relational ethics. Wendy J. Austin offers a good explanation of relational ethics from her perspective in the medical community:

> Relational ethics is a contemporary approach to ethics that situates ethical action explicitly in relationship. If ethics is about how we should live, then it is

> essentially about how we should live together. Acting ethically involves more than resolving ethical dilemmas through good moral reasoning; it demands attentiveness and responsiveness to our commitments to one another, to the earth, and to all living things. Ethics is about our interdependency as well as our freedom, our emotions as well as our reason, and our unique situation as well as our human commonalities. It involves finding the fitting responses to our ethical questions. . . .
>
> The answer to "How should I act?" is discovered not solely by oneself but rather in dialogue with others. We cannot know ahead of time, and with great certainty, how we should act. This does not mean that "everything is relative" or that "anything goes." Rather, it is acknowledged that we need to be sensitive to the whole of a given situation, to be inclusive in our dialogue about it, and to be aware of the effect of our contributions on it.[19]

Relational ethics speaks not of an absence of moral standards, but to the need to be in consultation with others to determine best courses of action. Postmodern ethics (of which relational ethics is one model) do not necessarily require a change in standards so much as a change in how we arrive at those standards, in how we understand language to bear truth, and in how we encourage others to do share our perspectives. In many situations moral answers seem clear. Even for most people who do not believe in transcendent values and who are reluctant to judge others, some situations are just wrong: racism, domestic violence, child abuse, murder, greed, oppression, and so on. A Jewish friend once commented that having 613 commandments gives clarity for ethics—you know what the law says so you do it automatically—and this frees one to concentrate on difficult ethical issues not covered by the laws. Austin herself notes that there are "some critics who wonder whether relational ethics means that it takes two to be ethical. This is not the case. There is, however, recognition that the individual learns to be ethical in relationships with others."[20]

Of course relationships can become a value unto themselves. Ronald J. Allen gives the following poignant example: "Some people—especially young adults—are highly relational. Their lives center on relationships and doing things together. As one of the twenty-somethings in one of our households says, 'We're all about relationship.' The preacher needs to help such folk recognize that not all relationships—and not all forms of community—embody God's intent for all to live together in inclusive well-being."[21]

To be heard by today's generations, here are some relational practices preachers might follow in dealing with ethical and moral goodness:

(1) Pay attention to the particularity of things, to the distinctiveness of situations and circumstances (Derrida's differance). Don't generalize as

modern preachers did, using sweeping assessments to classify and sterotype groups in society. Instead, raise moral or social issues by focusing on individual stories or case studies from diverse settings, respecting confidentiality. Empathize with the people involved, don't stand in judgment over them or hold them to ridicule. That does not mean you should condone bad actions, but rather treat the people as human beings whose failures have costs for them as well as for others. For example, if a preacher wants to preach on apathy, it would be unwise to single out any one group of people as apathetic. Instead, tell a couple of stories that lead to deeper insight about apathy, perhaps one about a teenager who has given up trying to get a summer job after many attempts, and one about the children of a senior citizen whose children seem not to care about her.

(2) Use narrative to create a sense of real people involved and avoid creating stereotypes. Sometimes just an odd detail in a case study can add realism, like the medical doctor who smells of cigarette smoke: A stereotype about doctors is broken.

(3) Keep the whole community in mind when talking about tough issues. Emphasize community engagement and resolution of issues over the preacher coming up with an independent solution in a sermon.

(4) On making moral and ethical decisions, stress congregational interdependency over individualism, relationships over isolation, and community discernment over independence.

(5) Modern notions of unity were static and stressed conformity and identical understanding. Contemporary understandings of unity can be fluid, dynamic, and embrace the unity that comes with differences in Christ held together by the Holy Spirit. What these understandings will be cannot be said apart from the communities that must engage the issues.

Can preachers still mention evil and sin and get a hearing? In fact, some post-structuralist philosophers are better at naming evil than many church leaders, and we could imitate their speech. Michel Foucault (d. 1984) could be speaking of sin, "My point is not that everything is bad, but that everything is dangerous.... If everything is dangerous, then we always have something to do."[22] Philosopher Jean Baudrillard, who often seemed outrageous for his opinions, asked what happened to evil and concluded that it had gone everywhere in Western society, because it is denied.[23] Evil exists in the "virtual consensus that prevails" about its denial,[24] in "the discourse of the Good" that masks it,[25] like our use of euphemisms.[26]

Relational ethics accentuates connections between things, interdependency and getting the whole picture. Relational ethics is a natural fit for the church. Modern ethics tended to be laws and abstract ideas, but in the current milieu it is possible to reconceive of ethics in terms of relationships, most importantly with God.

Theologian Martha Stortz shows us how we might speak in terms of this relationship. She contrasts the world's peace and justice (good 1) with the peace and justice of Christ (good 2):

> Peace no longer rests in the removal of settlements or the establishment of an independent security force or the end of genocide, all of which would be good outcomes. The world's peace can only be defined negatively by what is not happening. Biblical peace has the richness of relationship to a Person, who is himself the "Prince of Peace" (Isa 9:6). It's a lot harder to say what this looks like. The only thing to do is follow this person around. . . . Biblical justice comes to us not merely as the end of injustice but through the richness of relationship to a Person, who wears righteousness as a belt (Isa 11:5). In his work among us, Christ took up our sin and gave us the righteousness of God, a life-saving transaction that Luther calls "the happy exchange," and the Apostle Paul describes in full: "God caused the one who didn't know sin to be sin for our sake so that through him we could become the righteousness of God" (2 Cor 5:21). Through faith in Christ and baptism into his body, we are made not simply righteous but "the righteousness of God."[27]

Good acts are empowered by God. Discussion of ethics in the sermon can be not just a list of shoulds, musts, and have tos. It can be form of faith witness. Jesus said, "Without me, you can't do anything" (John 15:5). Paul stressed, "Not that we are competent of ourselves to claim anything as coming from us; our competence is from God" (2 Cor 3:5 NRSV). Ethical laws can be turned over using our process of inversion to discover what they say about God. In fact, to find good news in a moralistic reading of James, that practice is almost required. In doing good we participate in God's restoration of all creation, the making of all things new in Christ.

Chapter Six

What Easter Deconstructs (Practice)

In this chapter we turn to the theopoetic practice of goodness. Good Friday and Easter is the second big gospel celebration upon which we focus, a key historic event upon which the faith is based. With the chapter on Christmas we emphasized beginnings, the beginning of Jesus's story, faith, and sermons. Here we focus largely on the content of faith and the sermon. Easter is the central event of the church. It defines who we are as a people of a loving God. In the cross and resurrection we see a God who in Christ "emptied himself / by taking the form of a slave / and by becoming like human beings. / When he found himself in the form of a human, / he humbled himself by becoming obedient to the point of death, / even death on a cross" (Phil 2:7-8). This is goodness. Every Sunday we mark God's goodness, the forgiveness for us to be counted as good, and the power for us to do good on behalf of one another.

Easter and Preaching

Every Sunday is a little Easter. Lent is supposed to last forty days to mark the length of Jesus's temptation in the wilderness but the season of Lent in the church year is more than forty days. That is because every Sunday is a celebration of Easter goodness. Each of the four Gospels leads to the resurrection, and the resurrection is not only the end of every Gospel but also the effective ending of every text taken from any of the Gospels—they are all to be read in the light of both the beginning and the end of the story. The Gospel stories gain their meaning in relation to the identity of Christ as the one who lives now, risen from the dead. We could be even more bold. The resurrection and what leads up to the Second Coming is the effective ending of every biblical text even beyond the Gospels. In a sense, then, every biblical text, no matter how terrifying or tragic, has a good ending. The ending is God wins.

Because here we look to Easter, we also look to the Second Person of the Trinity and to the second moment of the Christian story that needs a much higher profile in the regular preaching of the church. In the modern age, Christian identity was largely assumed in churches. In the postmodern age, and if the church is to welcome postmodern difference, Christian identity and discipleship cannot be taken for granted. The cross and resurrection need in some way to be in focus in every sermon to help shape identity. This is not to assert mere propositions every week to the effect that Jesus lives; it is to invite people into the poetry of Easter, such that they encounter through our stories and words the living Christ, by the power of the Holy Spirit. The goodness of God each week is presented in current situations and events that contain the distinctive fingerprints of the God who saves most distinctively by raising from death. Poetry is often the best way to speak of this reality.

Deconstruction is not a beautiful word to my ears. It is musical in French but in English, it has a hard, ugly edge and all the poetry of a concrete block. It becomes a slightly more beautiful word, however, when we associate it with Good Friday and Easter. If I were to preach an Easter sermon, I would need a theme sentence that has Gardner's notions of beauty, it needs to be interesting, memorable, and worthy of being revisited. It also needs to focus on a good, empowering action of God. In the context of these pages I choose "Jesus destroys death" and I will try to develop it using the notion of deconstruction—a word I might not even mention in a church setting unless the people knew what it meant.

The church itself seems to be in a period of decline and deconstruction: How will we attract more youth or young families? What about the future? What about the roof? What about the Sunday school? There are yet deeper questions. When we consider the places of death in the world, in our communities, in our own life, does it seem that death often reigns supreme? Is the stone on the burial tomb unmoved? Or has it been rolled away?

Every Easter, churches typically begin the service with a litany, "Christ is risen. He is risen indeed. Hallelujah!" It is supposed to sound good. In a way, it is unfortunate that Easter services begin that way, because when the congregation says "Hallelujah!" as one voice, at least in most Euro-American churches, it almost always does so in monotone, the result is a flat, depressed hallelujah with no capital H. It is hallelujah recalled from dim memory, as history, as a minor event, if you say so, or if we must. It seems more like an okay event rather than one that defines the essence of goodness itself. The way some of us say hallelujah we might just as well be at someone's funeral, perhaps our own, we sound that dead. At the beginning of the Easter service it is as though we sit at the breakfast table and someone says, "the toast is up, hallelujah," or "Sally is up, hallelujah." We are talking about Jesus, who is up from the dead! Many of the people who attend Easter services were not there on Good Friday, indeed, many have not been in attendance since Christmas. How can they be expected to say hallelujah like they mean it? They may not even know that Jesus died.

Problematize a Sermon

Hallelujah acknowledges goodness and gets volume in relation to Good Friday. As Ron Allen poetically says, "Christ is on the cross because that is where humanity is."[1] The resurrection can only speak in relation to the crucifixion. John Donne knew this. Good Friday, 2013, was the four hundredth anniversary of his writing "Good Friday, 1613. Riding Westward," a poem that marks his decision to enter the Church of England priesthood. Donne thinks of Christ rising on the cross and dying at Calvary and compares him to the sun: "There I should see a Sunne, by rising set, / And by that setting endlesse day beget."[2] By combining Good Friday and Easter his words gain power. In many ways we live in a Good Friday world, because so often sin, evil, and death seem to rule. It seems anything but good. *Seems* is a key word to use when describing events around us in preaching, "It seems like death rules, it seems like the powers and principalities have the final say . . ." However, *seems,* like Good Friday, harbors a larger, much brighter truth.

On Good Friday death seems to destroy Jesus, but on Easter Jesus destroys death. As soon as one says *Good Friday,* its binary opposite kicks in: The good and the bad of the day start to interact. We humans did the math, 1 + 1 = our need for a Savior, and we did not like it, so we killed Jesus. When we consider the torture Jesus suffered, the depth of human wrong, and the hideous injustice of that event and continuing present day events like it, *Bad Friday* seems right. The theme sentence on Easter gets at the good. Jesus destroyed death. By God's grace, when death sought the final, singular, totalizing word, its opposite rose up. Life itself would not be silenced. In relation to death, Jesus is the "trace" that cannot be erased.

The power of evil begins to unravel like a knitted sweater, snagged as it is on the nails of the cross. That is the poetry. God does not allow evil's finest expression to reign. The cross is emptied of its ultimate power as surely as the tomb is emptied of its ability to confine Jesus's body. God's love permanently defers the meaning evil sought.

That is the poetry. God does not allow evil's finest expression to reign.

The Good Friday and Easter sermons can be thought of as two parts of a single sermon. There may be no other regular sermons in the life of the church of which this can be said. Math says "death seems to win," and poetry says "God wins." The two are in conversation with each other, each deconstructing the other. Both need to be heard. Each is amplified by the other. Each becomes more credible in opposition. The decisive movement, however, is from Good Friday to Easter, from math to poetry. Conceived as two parts of the weekly sermon, death is present but its ultimate power is gone. Death now is but a shadow of itself. God is still in control. Injustice is here, but God's justice is already breaking in. Goodness reigns. Every day becomes a little Easter.

A friend I will name Peter, who looks like Ernest Hemingway, spoke of growing up. He said his mother, Hazel, had been a devout Roman Catholic and had a bad marriage. She divorced and remarried, but in the eyes of the church at that time, she was considered to be a fallen woman, so the family never again set foot in the church. In fact this friend did not even know his mother had been married previously, until he found three photographs of her with another man who also looked liked like Ernest Hemingway, one a wedding picture, one a formal portrait, and the third a picture of them in the Alps. He discovered not only that his mother had been married before but also that the dear man he thought was his father was his stepfather, and that his biological father was the man in the picture. When Peter was thirteen years old they moved across the street from an Anglican church. A friend became a crucifer, someone who carries the cross in the liturgy, so Peter thought he would like to do that as well. Other friends were in the youth group, so he joined that. One day he came home and the Anglican priest had crossed the road and was sitting on the back porch talking with his mother. *Oh, oh,* he thought, *I must be in trouble.* The visit went on for several hours. *I must be in serious trouble.* That was the day Peter's mother returned to church. Peter says, when that priest crossed the road, God crossed the road to fetch his Mom.[3]

The Hallelujah of Easter is in response to God's goodness. God wins; we and our sinful ways do not. Or better said, God wins and therefore we win. *Hallelujah* is not a wimp word or weasel word; it is a lithe, full-bodied, athletic, and energetic Olympic word. *Hallelujah* works out at the health club. It is a gymnastics word, a backflip word, a pole-vaulting word, a spin-on-your-head kind of word, not a crawl-on-your-belly kind of word. We need altitude when we say it, the kind that words like *cool, amazing,* or *awesome* often have when uttered while watching snowboarders do their soaring flips off enormous jumps. *Hallelujah* is from the Hebrew words *Halle,* meaning praise, and *Jah*, short for Yahweh, God's name. Praise God. We should say Hallelujah with the tone and enthusiasm we use to shout at the best shots in ice hockey or tennis. At the end of the Easter service we say our best Hallelujahs. There they are like helium balloons launched to the heavens. The congregation has had a chance to get to the tomb and discover it is empty. They say it like they mean it.

Give People Good Roles to Play in the Story

Why would people in church bother to say Hallelujah? There may be no good reason if they are in church just as observers or onlookers. Were it not for the sermon they might remain as just that. However, the sermon seeks to enroll all listeners as participants in a drama that gets acted out in various scenes each week throughout the year in preaching. The modern era thought of sermons as offering ideas to listeners, but in the postmodern we are better to think of the sermon offering roles to play in their lives. For instance, at Christmas, perhaps they come with the shepherds and the Magi to pay homage and worship the newborn king. In the Easter story, they may come as Peter or John, or as the women to the tomb, or disciples in the locked room, or as witnesses to one of Jesus's resurrection appearances. The biblical story through preaching becomes their story in some way, so that by the end of the Easter service they might say the words poet George Herbert addressed to the risen Christ: "With Thee / O let me rise."[4]

Believers have a role in the sermon. Two writers in particular help preachers with this notion. Kevin J. Vanhoozer argues that the drama of doctrine involves "how best to perform one's discipleship."[5] The scriptural story of redemption is the beginning of their script. Christian performances must be "creative as well as faithful."[6] The performer recognizes God as the author of the drama,[7] and one's individual task is "to transpose the drama of redemption into the present."[8]

Samuel Wells takes a similar track. He claims that good acts happen more by habit than by making decisions in the crisis of the moment. Worship, baptism, and Eucharist shape the virtuous habits of the church. Imagination helps people to improvise ethical behavior. First they need to "over-accept" their circumstance, look for ways to turn them to positive advantage for good.[9] Second, they need to "reincorporate" those individuals who are on the outside into a larger narrative, not as problems for which allowances must be made, but as gifts of God.[10] The church needs to "stretch its imagination to the full dimensions and cosmic scope of the Christian story."[11] Wells critiques ethics for accepting the limits of situations as though they are given, and thinking of God as a kind of bonus or gift. He wants the givens (the limits) to be received as gifts, and wants people to think of God as the given, the one who is in control.[12] People begin living the biblical script in the sermon, and God continues to open pathways to good acts of ministry for them in the future.

Get to the Good News

It is possible to sit in the pews and think of Easter only as history or "just a story." The goodness of God becomes apparent when God's saving action in the biblical text is transposed into our day. Walk now the morning path that Mary Magdelene walked through the garden with crocuses and lilies in bloom, to a cliff where many tombs are carved out, one above another. One tomb has its stone rolled back, exposing a simple stone ledge inside. She fetches Peter and John, who rush in and hurry home, but Mary remains standing there. She looks in the tomb and sees two angels, and a gardener approaches of whom she asks, "Sir, if you have carried him away, tell me where you have put him and I will get him" (John 20:15). At this point, Jesus reveals his identity. "Mary," he says, "Don't hold on to me, for I haven't yet gone up to my Father. Go to my brothers and sisters and tell them, 'I'm going up to my Father and your Father, to my God and your God' " (John 20:16-17). In going, Mary becomes the first preacher of Christ.

What makes this present visit to the tomb special is that as people enter the tomb of Jesus's death, they enter also the tomb of bad things in their own lives. The sermon names some of them: Someone sees images of the hospital bed where a friend lies confined by a long illness. Someone else sees the schoolyard where her child is daily bullied. Another person is at the graveside of a loved one. Others see the face of a friend they cheated or a marriage that failed. Some see the latest mass murder in the news, countries at war, places of famine and floods: the death of dreams, the death of innocence, the death of hope.

These are places Jesus's cross now stands tall. The empty tomb says "death no more." Something startlingly new is at play. It is not mainly a matter of right creeds and doctrines, or even of faith seeking understanding, or weighing pros and cons; it is a matter of experiencing the power of death gone, Jesus in the Spirit, testified to in scripture, alive in the present. Paul says, "knowledge of God's mystery... [is] Christ himself" (Col 2:2 NRSV). Where might we look for Jesus's resurrection? Most surely in the places of suffering and death.

Good Acts

A friend said, "It is harder to be a believer now than in biblical times, when God and God's prophets were more present and obvious." Is that correct? Scholars tell us that Mark originally ended his gospel at 16:8 with no resurrection appearances. Perhaps this was not because there were none to report, but because there were too many. The angel says to the women, "Go, tell his disciples, especially Peter, that he is going ahead of you into Galilee. You will see him there, just as he told you" (16:7). Mark did not need to describe the resurrection appearances because the same words are true for all disciples, even today, "He has gone ahead of you into whatever trouble you face. You will see him there, just as he told you." John says at the end of his Gospel, "Jesus did many other things as well. If all of them were recorded, I imagine the world itself wouldn't have enough room for the scrolls that would be written" (21:25; see 20:30-31). He is not talking about a scarcity of appearances, but a plethora of them, so numerous that they cannot be counted. It makes sense, given what Jesus said in Matthew 28:20, "Look, I myself will be with you every day until the end of this present age," and in John 14:16, "I will ask the Father, and he will send another Companion, who will be with you forever."

Maybe we do not live in an age of miracles. I tend to think, however, that a miracle is any act of God, and evidence of God seems to be everywhere. Any act of good is evidence of God. Any act of righteousness, justice, peace, hospitality, selflessness, and love is a resurrection act. Sally Brown gives an example of such a life-giving act:

> In an East coast city, a middle-aged couple stepped through an open church door and sank gratefully into a back pew of the church's large, quiet sanctuary. Only recently, the congregation had agreed to leave the church open all day to the public. A church member arranging chancel flowers noticed the couple's stricken faces and asked if she could help. She learned this was not their church—or even their town. Early that morning police had notified them that their daughter, a college student in town, had been killed in an automobile accident. They had driven half the night, numb and exhausted. Without a church of their own, they had no friends in this city and did not know where to turn.
>
> In that critical time, the congregation provided friendship, hospitality for arriving family members, and pastoral care. Days later, the doors of the church were thrown open to hundreds who attended the memorial service for the couple's daughter. Months later, the couple returned to share in the annual All Saints' requiem service. Critical moments are openings to the movement of the Spirit.[13]

The effect of such a story can be to give any congregation a bigger vision of themselves and what they can do.

A student preached a story about Martin, who was the older of the two children in a family that had always been financially comfortable. He was just graduating from university when neither of his parents were able to work any longer, and he was the only one who could be the breadwinner. Martin was rejected for jobs for which he was well qualified. He wondered what purpose God had for him when he landed his dream job with the company he most wanted to work for. The only problem was that it did not nearly pay enough for him to maintain his family. Martin got up his courage and went in and explained his situation to his new boss and asked if there was any way he could earn more money. It turned out that his boss had had a similar experience, "I had to support my family when I graduated." He told him he would get back to Martin, and when he did it was to tell him that they would pay him an additional twenty thousand dollars.[14]

Some people might not tell that story lest it suggest if we have enough faith, God will solve all of our economic worries. Derrida would call that a totalizing claim, closing conversation. It implies poverty is lack of faith. That red flag is deconstruction at its best: What the story does not say it ends up saying and should avoid. Before walking that story to the trash bin, ask: What if Martin had not been offered more money? Would that mean

God did not care about Martin and his family? Theopoetry not only might tell the story but go on to imagine other kinds of evidence of God's love that might be found even without the extra funds offered by the boss.

A preacher never just tells a good story. Stories are not heard on their own. They are heard intertextually, in relation to the other elements of the surrounding sermon. Other things are always going on beyond the story itself. It is placed alongside these other stories, ideas, images, and emotions and it is interpreted and judged in relation to them. Every story acts as a metaphor of something in the sermon. And every metaphor has what Paul Ricoeur once called a yes and a no (in these postmodern times we might say every comment has a yes and no). "The snow is a field of diamonds," has a no, snowflakes are not gems, and a yes, each flake glitters in the sun. Wise preachers will anticipate that every story functions like a metaphor and will ask, What is the yes and what is the no? And they will work to minimize the no. The yes needs to be louder for effective communication. The story of a father who loved his teenaged daughter so much he gave her an expensive car has a yes, that is generous, and a no, that may not be what is best for her, and the no in this case may be louder. The story of a mother who loved her son so much she gave up her holiday in Spain to spend his birthday with him as he recovers in hospital has a louder yes than no.

Good Words of Proclamation

Proclamation takes the sermon beyond teaching about the good news into the hallelujah zone, to an experience of God speaking to the hearers. *Benediction* means speaking the good, the diction of the *bene.* Benediction is one kind of proclamation, and like the benediction at the end of a worship service, proclamation usually comes toward the end of the sermon. Celebration at the end of many African American sermons is often proclamation. Proclamation is in itself a momentary in-breaking of the realm or kingdom of God, for even this moment will die. As Jesus said, "Heaven and earth will pass away, but my words will certainly not pass away" (Luke 21:33). The preacher talks but the people in faith hear another voice. Where death once reigned, Christ now stands alive:

> To the person afraid of life, the risen Christ says, "Do not be afraid, for I have redeemed you; / I have called you by name, you are mine. / When you pass through the waters, I will be with you; / and through the rivers, they shall not overwhelm you." (Isa 43:1-2 NRSV)

To the person going through painful divorce,
he says, "I will always be with you." (Matt 28:20, paraphrased)
To the ones who mourn he says,
"I will wipe every tear from your eye." (Rev 21:4, paraphrased)
To the guilty he says,
"Repent, and receive the good news of forgiveness." (comment based on Luke 24:47)
To those needing justice, he says,
it will "roll down like waters, / and righteousness like an ever-flowing stream" (Amos 5:24 NRSV)
To those facing war he says,
"Come to me, all you who are weary and are carrying heavy burdens, and I will give your rest." (Matt 11:28 NRSV)
To the dying one he says,
"In my Father's house are many dwelling places . . . [and] I go to prepare a place for you." (John 14:2 NRSV)

If you have recovered from a long illness, Christ stood by your bed.
If you have experienced emotional healing, Christ laid his hands on you and healed you. If you have found peace where you expected destruction, know that Christ went ahead of you.
If you have found community in the church, the Holy Spirit has visited you, you have found your Maker, met your Savior.
And so it is that on this day, Scripture attests what experience affirms and we say Christ is Risen. The tomb is empty.[15]

Proclamation is God's good word spoken in the person of God directly to the people. It can be a small or large part of every sermon. It has the potential to disturb, inspire, console, empower, bless, heal, and even raise the dead. It leads listeners again to our Hallelujah word. If Easter was just history, we could not say Hallelujah, or we would say it only in the most depressed kind of way. But when we know that Jesus has destroyed death, *Hallelujah* is a dancing word. It is a word we want to sing and shout because the best news in the world has come to us. We do not need to be into handclapping and foot stomping—though that might help—in order to say Hallelujah the way it is meant to be said, like we mean it, like we know it and can show it. Christ is risen. He is risen for me. He is risen for you. A new world is at hand; a new creation has begun; death has been defeated. Hallelujah, hallelujah, hallelujah.

Good Motivation

What gets you excited about the faith? Martin Luther wrote, "If there is anything in us, it is not our own; it is a gift of God. But if it is a gift of God, then it is entirely a debt one owes to love, that is, the law of Christ. And if it is a debt owed to love, then I must serve others with it, not myself."[16] John Calvin spoke about the third use of the law as a kind of grace that excites the believer to obedience. What gets you excited to do God's will? What makes you passionate about the gospel? What will get your people excited to do God's bidding?

A teacher of preaching once said that he did not believe in the use of contemporary stories in preaching. My colleague quipped, "Is that because you don't think there is any evidence of God in our time?" and told this story:

> Recently a woman named Laurie Jones joined Bethany Church. She had been abused and neglected by her family. Later she was abandoned by her husband and left with two small children. Then one day she wandered into Bethany Church. People in this church "did everything for me" as she put it. The deacons paid her heating bill several times. Someone else in church babysat for her when the kids got the flu. And since she couldn't afford a car, another person in church brought her grocery shopping each week. On top of that, there always seemed to be a listening ear at Bethany Church. Some people griped a bit. "Why bother?" they said, "She isn't even a member."
>
> But several years after she began coming to church, she decided formally to make profession of faith in Jesus Christ and to join Bethany. That Sunday she also informed the congregation of something else. People at Bethany didn't know whether to laugh or cry. Laurie told the congregation that in the past week she had legally changed her name to Laurie Bethany. With tears in her eyes she told them, "You people are the only family that I ever had."

Such stories offer glimpses of God at work, evidence of resurrection power in our midst. They serve to motivate listeners to conform their lives to God's purposes.

The stories we look for are not all sweetness and light. Stories about brokenness and hardship, illuminated by moments of insight to the divine, have a special kind of authenticity. Richard Rohr muses about how the most we can do by way of good is to "second God's motion": "The path of descent is the path of transformation. Darkness, failure, relapse, death, and woundedness are our primary teachers, rather than ideas or doctrines. . . . The healthy religious person is the one who allows God to do the saving and the leading, while I do my little part to bring up the rear. . . . God is always the initiator and mover. All we do is second the motion."[17] For good news, we do not just forget about the death of a child, the bad breakup of a relationship or being fired from a job. Like stones becoming sand, in preaching, prayer, worship, and song the bad things lose their power over listeners and they are given what they need to go on.

Still, some stories can get sentimental. Kenneth Meyers says with humor, "sentimentality is loving something more than God does."[18] A great guitar can be poorly played and a great story can be poorly told. A sentimental story evokes emotion but does not stand up to critical thinking. "Happily ever after" is sentimental because life is not like that. Acknowledge that some bad stuff remains and your story will gain authenticity. Show healing in the midst of woundedness, joy in the midst of sorrow, Easter in the center of what often seems like a Good Friday world—note the word *seems.* Jeremy Begbie says Christian sentimentalism "arises from a premature grasp for Easter morning... [in the] irreversible sequence of victory over evil."[19] Sentimentality, he says: evades or trivializes evil,[20] cannot engage "in depth of another's pain as *pain,*"[21] and fails to move people to "appropriate costly action"[22] in serving others. Begbie's words hint a good movement of the sermon: Treat sin and evil seriously, enter the real pain of others, move to God's actions in the biblical text, and point to the mission the congregation might engage empowered by the cross.

Good contemporary stories point two ways: back to the resurrection as a source of empowerment and forward to the end of time when all of God's promises will be seen to be true. That is why the Second Coming is so important for faith, as we will see in the next section. It is not mainly a matter of rational closure to a rigid system of thought; it is an opening to the goodness and wonders of God. Begbie says, "The fulfillment toward which the resurrection points us, and which it anticipates, is not a mere restoration of a previous order, a return to the *status quo ante* of Eden; it is not only a recovery of what is lost but a *radical recreation of all things.*"[23] In other words, there is a time when goodness will be all in all.

There is a time when goodness will be all in all.

God is good. Every Sunday a miracle takes place in preaching, a sermon is born, God speaks, God acts, a new creation is ushered in, communities are transformed in Christ's image, and Christ kneels in service to the world.

Part III

Truth and Transformation

Chapter Seven

Truth as Event (Theory)

Beautiful preaching deals in goodness, and it also needs to be true, real, authentic. If it lacks reality, if it seems like fantasy or "just a story," it is worth nothing. Preachers of my grandparents' generation were confident in ways few preachers can afford to be today. They were confident in their ability to preach objective truth and in the openness of their congregations to receive it. Faith was mostly individualistic and preaching was for saving souls. Social matters beyond outreach to the poor, sick, and in prison were considered politics not religion. Faith was based in reason and knowledge, young people were taught the meaning of the creeds, and doctrinal or moral truths were the common focus of sermons. That age trusted a correspondence model of truth where propositions and points were believed to correspond with external and universal truth.

Truth Today

Preachers cannot safely have that confidence today because notions of truth have changed. Former notions of truth now are often seen as pretentious, as Stanley J. Grenz notes, "Postmoderns denounce the pretense of those who claim to view the world from a transcendent vantage point from which they are able to speak imperiously to and on behalf of all humankind."[1] As Derrida famously said, "There is nothing outside of the text,"[2] in other words, there is no meaning outside of human language. Truth claims are dismissed as easily as weather reports. Pontius Pilate could have been postmodern when he questioned Jesus at his trial, "What is truth?" Pilate is now enrolled as a student in the seminary, and is teaching some classes. People ask "what truth?" since truth is hard to find; "whose truth?" since truth seems relative; and "which truth?" since many truths may apply. Truth is typically no longer conceived as an abstract external reality or an idea in the mind of God. We no longer divide the individual into mind, body, and soul, as though they are separate entities. Reason and logic are no longer prized above all else. Filling the mind with correct teachings is no longer considered on its own to be the best way to form disciples of Jesus Christ. Wisdom has become more important than cognitive knowledge, in part because wisdom speaks of integration of various ways of knowing and different kinds of intelligence.[3]

The church in the modern era tended to assume its version of truth was what mattered. Truth was static. History was understood as fact, not as an interpretation or a rendering of events into a coherent plot or narrative. Truth, like God, was thought to be unchanging: What was true then is true now and will be true in the future. Present context was largely irrelevant because truth applied equally everywhere. Moreover, preaching was conceived in large measure as the preacher getting the truth right and the people somehow absorbing those truths for themselves.

Now truth is fluid. It changes with context. Humans are aware of the limits of language in bearing truth, and language is not the certain and precise tool we once thought it to be. Truth is poetic. Words generate perceptions of what is real that are not identical to things or ideas. There is no fixed one-to-one correspondence between reality and words. No fully formed external reality is identical to our formulations. Context and perspective shape everything. History is seen by many to be a kind of fiction; it shapes and selects the information it renders, but no one uncontested version of the whole is possible. We can no longer even be certain about what is history in history.

People today tend to be skeptical; they do not just accept what the preacher says is true because authority now tends to be in question. What might be true must make sense; it must have some practical benefit in their lives. The focus of preaching in such a milieu is not just the preacher getting things right, arguably the focus should be on equipping the people to speak about their faith for themselves.

Contemporary Claims about Truth

Preaching in postmodern times requires that preachers be alert to how language operates and how things have changed. Preachers who simply claim "this is the truth" are likely to be met with "that's your version of truth." Preachers can still speak about truth, but they cannot bring all of their modern presumptions about truth to the table and expect a good reception. Truth has been used as a shield to justify many abuses by the church in the past: What the church, priest, or minister says is necessarily true. Here are ten claims about truth in the contemporary world that affect how preachers read the Bible, interpret it for today, and are heard in these times:

(1) Truth as a concept is not necessarily a concern of the current age. As David J. Lose observes, "Postmodernity at its best stands against modernity's penchant to quash dissenting voices in its relentless quest for order, stability, unity, and certainty. At its worst postmodernity loses all confidence in *any* truth or conviction beyond its own pessimistic views on the absence of truth and the futility of conviction."[4] Cynicism and nihilism ironically tend to be neutral in political perspective, any meaning is worthy of deconstruction. Knowledge, power, and truth are seen politically: who says one thing is to be valued more than something else and to whose advantage?

A lesson for preachers: Instead of making appeals that imply "this is the truth so listen to it," take time to communicate in what ways something strikes you as the truth. Give good reasons for thinking something is true.

(2) Truth is often transformative, and it is valued. It changes how we think of things. It often elevates standards. Truth is appreciated for what it effects, what it does, what benefits it brings, what useful outcome it produces. With regard to faith, truth must offer outcomes that matter to many people and not just answer questions people have not asked. Concern is not so much for what happens at the end of life as it is transformation of life in the present, the end times breaking in now as justice, peace, mercy, love—renewed creation, the things that mark God's presence and eternal realm.

A lesson for preachers: Speak about truth not primarily as abstract ideas, but in terms of its effects, and what benefits it brings. For example, we spoke earlier about communicating faith to others not primarily on the basis that is true as an intellectual system, but because it offers beauty in life.

(3) Truth operates within human systems and relationships that help determine its effects.[5] Truth in courts is what the rules of law are able to establish; in politics it is what persuades voters; in business it is what sells—lately many corporations have gone green, they want to be perceived in a certain way. Truth does not always operate as we would like, even in churches: A church board might decide not to speak out on a matter of social injustice because it might cause some controversy in the congregation. Comedians express cynicism about what passes for truth: The American Dialect Society chose Comedian Stephen Colbert's coined word *truthiness*

as the 2005 Word of the Year, "the quality of preferring concepts or facts one wishes to be true, rather than concepts or facts known to be true."[6]

A lesson for preachers: Do not assume that truth means only one thing, or that there is only one truth. Rather, acknowledge that there are many truths today, everyone has their own version, and that not all of them we would want to affirm.

(4) Truth, like other values, is a social construct. The meaning or truth of a biblical text may vary depending upon setting: A literature class may focus on meanings the church does not hold, like that by riding into Jerusalem Jesus committed suicide. Meaning depends upon the lens used to find it. Liberation criticism produces a critique of political or economic powers, postcolonial criticism uncovers vestiges of colonialism, feminist criticism discloses biases against women, and so on. Increasingly, historical and social analyses focus on issues of gender, class, sexuality, race, and ethnicity. Each instrument claims to determine the most important elements of a text.

A lesson for preachers: Even with those truths we might want to affirm, do not assume that all listeners understand them the same way. Truth depends on perspective, and by acknowledging that from time to time, listeners can come to trust the preacher to respect other perspectives on truth.

(5) Truth is fluid. Angélique Du Toit says, "Postmodernism argues that meaning is transitory and constantly evolving and therefore has no permanence of substance. The emphasis is on the joint authorship of meaning between the signifier and the signified."[7] In other words, meaning is generated in interaction of symbols and contexts in the moment. Truth is composed by the speaker and understood by different people in different ways in different social settings. We see this with individuals on the Internet who are able to take on different identities in virtual communities, each of them seemingly "true."[8]

A lesson for preachers: What is true needs to be negotiated with the congregation in the course of a sermon. This negotiation is not an intellectual debate; it is rather a process of making meaning together by bringing the poetry of scripture into relationship with the issues involved and thinking them through afresh.

(6) Truth is an event more than a fixed notion. It exists as moments of insight or interpretation. It is fleeting. Ability to possess truth is limited given that everything is an interpretation, language is inexact, meanings and referents are unstable, and everything depends on perspective. Preachers need think twice about saying "the meaning of this text is" or "history tells us," for as Kevin Vanhoozer explains, "For many postmodern interpreters,

there is not 'the meaning,' nor 'the past'; instead, there is 'my interpretation' or 'our interpretation' of these things."[9]

A lesson for preachers: Instead of thinking of truth as some abstract formulation that exists out there and that we are trying in the sermon to get right, think instead of the sermon in this moment as making truth. Preachers have long understood the sermon to exist as a moment in time. Preachers may carry that same notion over to truth as an event in time.

(7) Truth is relational. It is communal in its identity, shaped by the perspectives of the particular group of people. The church must place its message amongst many other claims about what is meaningful and important: Every app, ad, article, and program makes truth claims. Moreover, we all live by many stories, not just biblical ones: of our country, ancestors, immediate families, joys and sorrows, successes and failures, from the news, movies, Facebook, and so forth. The church's message does not stand independent of the times and cultures in which it is heard. The culture is part of the reality of any biblical text in this moment. It affects what the text says. Far from distorting or distracting from the text, culture makes interpretation necessary and possible.

A lesson for preachers: The truth of a sermon cannot be reduced to one set of ideas, as some preachers might try to do with sermon outline. The truth of a sermon is the whole sermon understood in terms of all the relationships involved. Its truths are unique for that moment, framed by the relationships of the particular biblical text to the people present, to the church context, and to the various settings and people with which the congregation connects in the culture at large. Preachers and people bring meanings to the sermon and take various meanings away.

(8) Truth is plural, not singular. Meaning is changing and does not say just one thing. Deconstruction points to what a text also says by its silence. Many different truths can exist alongside one another. The Bible has shown this: Proverbs 26:4 reads, "Don't answer fools according to their folly, / or you will become like them yourself," while 26:5 reads, "Answer fools according to their folly, / or they will deem themselves wise." They are both true; one does not exclude the other. Poet Margaret Avison observed about God's grace, "In the mathematics of God, there are percentages beyond one hundred."[10]

A lesson for preachers: Even the use of a theme sentence, as we advocate here, does not limit the truths the preachers may intend to speak or the truths the people may hear, whether the preacher intends them or not. People will have many interpretations of the sermon. The theme sentence simply is a guide people need to help them negotiate the truth for themselves that week; it helps them be able to make meaning from what is said.

(9) Truth is best uttered leaving some room for movement and participation. This guideline does not apply when warning a child that something is hot, but most of the time it does, for instance, when one seeks to influence the attitudes of another person. In modern times, truth was a simpler matter and hitting others over the head with it was thought to be good. Someone rightly said the world rarely yields to frontal assaults. Emily Dickinson said, "Tell all the truth but tell it slant / . . . The truth must dazzle gradually / Or every man be blind."[11] W. H. Auden might have read her poem when he composed, "Truth, like love and sleep, resents Approaches that are too intense."[12] Recently Eugene Peterson has likewise observed, "There are many occasions when the imperious or blunt approach honors neither our God nor our neighbor. Unlike raw facts, truth, especially personal truth, requires the cultivation of unhurried intimacies."[13] In other words, much truth requires poetry for expression. Truths about God are examples of this: We cannot speak of God to fullest effect without the poetry of the Bible.

A lesson for preachers: Theopoetic preachers will resist trying to summarize the sermon by reducing it to abstract propositional truths. That is what modern preachers sometimes did. There is no one meaning of a sermon; there is just what the preacher said through word and gesture. Even the preacher has no control over what is done with it, what meanings or truths are found there. The preacher can only try to communicate as clearly as possible, with as much unity and coherence as possible.

(10) Truth today is often recognized as authenticity and integrity: People long for authentic community, not just virtual or online connections. They seek hand-crafted foods and drinks, local produce, and quality goods. They want authentic relationships, people to be what they seem to be, organizations to be transparent. Authenticity and integrity may be new standards based in relationships whereby folks measure what was called truth.

A lesson for preachers: Classical rhetoric recognized the importance of a speaker's ethos or character in classical notions of persuasion. Today, persuasion by argument is seen as a holdover from the Enlightenment, and identification with what is said is favored over competitive ways of trying to score points. The integrity and faithfulness of a preacher is all the more important, seen not least in evidence that the preacher is well prepared.

Transforming Truth

Stories can be vehicles of truth that effect transformation. It is evident at several levels in the tragic story of the thirteen people killed and thirty-two wounded by Major Nidal Malik Hasan at Fort Hood, Texas, on November 5, 2009. Nader Hasan, a cousin of the killer, had a small criminal defense law firm in Fairfax Virginia. "Our phones went completely quiet, dead.... We relied on referrals. I lost dozens of prospective clients, and it still happens."[14] He wrestled with whether to speak out lest it bring more publicity, but he set up an organization against Islamic violence and dedicated to cooperation and understanding among patriotic American Muslims and non-Muslims.

Two years later, Kerry Cahill, the daughter of one of the men killed, met with Nader and decided to accept his invitation to sit on the board of the foundation. "We are both angry at the same thing," she said, "I am constantly reminded of a quote attributed to Edmund Burke: 'All that is necessary for the triumph of evil is that good men do nothing.'"[15] Every sermon should have stories that bear truth and potentially communicate God, thereby allowing for transformation of the hearers.

Metanarratives and Truth

The concept of truth is a problem today and so are metanarratives, thus preachers may feel doubly vulnerable since both truth and the Bible may seem undermined. *Metanarratives* is a fancy word for grand stories that shape cultures and determine social values. The overall Christian story as found in the Bible is a metanarrative. Eastern Orthodox theologian David Bentley Hart does what many scholars do; he defines modernity in terms of metanarrative: "The great project of 'modernity' (the search for comprehensive metanarratives and epistemological foundations by way of a neutral and unaided rationality, available to all reflective intellects, and independent of cultural and linguistic conditions) has surely foundered."[16] *Kerygma* is the Greek word for proclamation of the good news in Jesus Christ, and it refers to something related to metanarrative. The ecumenical creeds reflect the content of our overarching story or plot: God came in Jesus Christ to reconcile the world to God's ways.

The church listened with particular interest in 1979 when philosopher Jean-François Lyotard said, "I define *postmodern* as incredulity toward metanarratives."[17] He referred in particular to what he called "the Enlightenment narrative" in which knowledge is the hero and the plot moves toward the goal of universal peace.[18] The Enlightenment narrative found support in progress in the sciences.[19] It operated by consensus and made sense of society, and like the Christian story, it implied universal application and authority. It became the underlying truth against which societal knowledge was measured.

Metanarratives are coercive and have been used to control knowledge, people, and activities that do not fit. Lyotard's point was that metanarratives disregard differences and try to make one size fit all. They distort reality, they represent a modernist "nostalgia [for] the whole and the one."[20] They are "haunted by the paradisiac representation of a lost 'organic' society."[21] He argues that we do not need metanarratives in order to bond as a society. All we need are individual local narratives and what he calls language games. An example is the game of inquiry, in which social positions are already assigned: the one who asks, the one who responds, and "the referent asked about."[22] These language games generate dynamics of power, authority, and legitimation of each. They can be used to undermine metanarrative's attempts to make absolute universal claims. Metanarratives claim truth for all time, rather than in the moment as an event.

For many people, postmodern views have a redeeming social purpose. Walter Lowe credits deconstruction with protecting free speech.[23] Stuart Sim says that Enlightenment ideology since the eighteenth century "has striven to bring about emancipation of mankind from economic want and political oppression" but in time "came to oppress humankind, and to force it into certain set ways of thought and action not always in its best interests."[24] Sim actually fears the demise of the postmodern movement. He is alarmed at the persistence or reemergence of grand narratives, for instance in the response to 9/11 and in various kinds of religious and economic fundamentalism on the global stage: "We need postmodernism to combat this essentially regressive tendency.... The postmodern is... a positive aspect of our culture that deserves our support."[25]

Sim seems to ascribe to postmodernism a status as a movement (implying a unified worldview), something many would deny. If it is that, it is open to the same critique it offers: It becomes a saving metanarrative in danger of making the same totalizing claims as any other metanarrative. The death of the metanarrative is itself a metanarrative. Lyotard said as much when he acknowledged "the great narrative of the end of great narratives."[26]

Theopoetry and Truth

Theopoetry is a positive way for the church to respond to contemporary changes in understanding truth. To listen to the theorists, it might seem like preachers have only two choices: On the one hand, we can hold on to our metanarrative and the dogmatic, coercive, fixed worldview that accompanies it. On the other hand, we can throw out the metanarrative and adopt the skepticism and cynicism that dismisses meaning and truth.

> Theopoetry is a positive way for the church to respond to contemporary changes in understanding truth.

Universal, singular, or totalizing claims can be made as much by the cynic sipping a mocha java at Starbucks as by the Christian in a Bible class. Either approach can function as math, yes or no, my way or the highway. However, cynicism and dogmatism are not the only options.

How can preachers respond to the rejection of metanarratives, given that they have in fact been used to mask many sicknesses and sins? On the other hand, to let go of the Christian metanarrative would be a huge loss, because it can have a beauty of its own, a logic of correspondences that, if it does not give a full picture of all things, does a good job of communicating overall the beauty of God and the goodness of God's purposes.

Everything is open to interpretation. The Bible functions as a metanarrative not in itself, as a collection of many different stories, but when the Christian story is used to offer others only a yes or no choice, to quash their dissent, in effect to "lord it over those in [his] charge" (1 Pet 5:3 NRSV). From a theopoetic perspective, such a yes or no stance is a form of math that is neither desired or needed. We may differ with people, but do so in as loving and respectful a way as possible. Jesus did not come to lord it over or to condescend to others; he knelt and washed their feet. We may find in that a new model of lordship and relating. Language is key: We have to be aware of the soft underbelly of our words. We have to be humble, knowing our words are not the secure chains to anchored truths that modernists imagined. Meaning is momentary, like a budding flower.

Theopoetry does not escape the tentative nature of words. Not everything fits. Much is fragmentary. Much is ambiguous. Theopoetry embraces mystery. Propositional paths are built with words like paving stones, but theopoetry is sculpted with words that fall like snowflakes on the dark waters of a pond. Meaning is tentative, variegated, textured, layered, brief, kinetic, kinesthetic, diverse, ambiguous, metaphoric, plurivocal, open—it is not closed, certain, or fully controlled. It is fleeting and comes as an event. Decades ago, Archibald MacLeish wrote "a poem should not mean but be," and preaching moves in that direction. I. A. Richards, during the same time, wrote about how poetry differs from science in which rational thought is foremost:

> It is never what a poem says which matters, but what it *is*. The poet is not writing as a scientist. He uses these words because the interests which the situation calls into play combine to bring them, just in this form, into his consciousness as a means of *ordering, controlling and consolidating* the whole experience. The experience itself, the tide of impulses sweeping through the mind, is the source and sanction of the words. [They] will reproduce in [the reader's] mind a similar play of interests.[27]

Theopoetry engenders confidence in part because it creates an experience and allows room for the Spirit and hearers to participate. Tall buildings gain strength when designed to move in the wind; theopoetry similarly allows for the wind to blow. Math has a beauty of precision, but when that precision of symbols is sought on spiritual matters, it tends to distort. On such matters theopoetry is often the most precise language one can hope for.

The Christian story is in fact many stories—the Bible is an anthology. Differences matter and these stories do not all say the same thing. Many say contradictory things. In contrast to the faith and confidence of many psalms, there is the devastating prayer of rejection that is Psalm 88 and the vengeance of Psalm 109. Even our grasp on significant events, like the exact nature of Jesus's bodily resurrection, allows room for imagination. The Gospel writers struggle with how to speak of the disciples' experiences. No one biblical theology exists. To think there might be unifying themes was a modernist notion that crashed with the biblical theology movement in the 1960s.

The Christian story is a metanarrative but it is also exactly what Lyotard advocated as an alternative, many local or small stories. The small stories, the texts we preach week to week, are not lost in the whole. Preaching also includes the small stories from contemporary daily life. The Christian metanarrative can function not as a lock on the truth but as something that helps unlock perspectives on truth. Even in the modern era, many preachers understood that truth was not something one could own: God's will needs to be continually sought.

> The small stories, the texts we preach week to week, are not lost in the whole.

A modern Christian might say "I know the unchanging truth." By contrast, a theopoet might say, "I know the truth, but knowing it is not possessing it, controlling it, or knowing it completely." Knowing truth does not mean I can erase the mystery of God. It does not mean I have a certain amount of knowledge, like so many books lined up on a shelf or framed degree certificates on a wall. And it also does not mean that I know best—everyone has some experience of God whether they know it or not. It does mean that I have what I understand to be a relationship with the living God, whom I know best in Jesus Christ.

Theopoetics and God

Truth is an event, known by what it affects, shaped by communities, discerned in relationships, understood in context, and sought anew in each moment. From a theopoetic perspective, truth is an encounter with the living God. Any knowledge we have of truth arises from God's actions. This is what Kevin Vanhoozer means when he says that "theology's first principle is *God in communicative action.*"[28]

Anslem said theology is faith seeking understanding. Theopoetic sermons are faith seeking God. God's actions and person are the focus, and only secondarily are they information we try to get our minds around. We encounter God in life as a living reality, a being with personhood, who acts on our behalf in loving and saving ways. Revelation in the Bible sometimes does come as a fixed formula of words, like the Ten Commandments or the writing on the wall in Daniel 5, but most often revelation comes as encounter, like Mary had with the gardener when the tomb was empty (John 20:15). Divine words spoken are as fleeting as last Sunday's sermon. Their evanescent nature contributes to the event.

When Jesus says, "you will know the truth, and the truth will set you free" (John 8:32), the modernist mind thinks of cognate knowledge that may accumulate with a lot of hard work and study. The theopoet may think instead of relationship: "You will know me in walking with me, and in walking with me, you will find freedom." Doctrines or teaching of the church possess knowledge, while theopoetry points, indicates, describes, invites, and beckons to experience. Even at that, theopoetry draws on theology and doctrines, and the church needs dedicated scholars to think through the logical implications of its teachings for the pulpit. Where the modernist may seize on the truth as a fixed nature, the theopoet points to the fluid process of its generation in community, guided by the Spirit.

Here is a wonderful irony. The postmodern world largely rejects abstract transcendent notions of goodness and truth. It looks instead to relationships and contexts on a case-by-case basis. This denial and emphasis on relationships ironically can lead in preaching to more authentic focus on God because truth, as I understand it, is to be found in living relationship to God. Modern preachers might have insisted that truth exists somewhere "out there" as a fixed abstract transcendent reality, implanted in the universe by God at creation. Preachers today might feel threatened by the loss of that notion. However, preachers need not mourn it, especially since it can be replaced by what is arguably a better understanding: Truth is part of the nature of God. Truth is not so much implanted in creation as a universal abstract, it is rather who God is. We can know the truth, we just cannot know truth completely, or as Paul says, "Now we see through a glass, darkly; but then face to face" (1 Cor 13:12 KJV). We can know the truth, but truth is the living God, not a static entity somehow separate from God.

Unlike in modern times, no one can have a corner on truth, because no one can possess God. When people have claimed to have a corner on truth, they have often used it to oppress others. David Bentley Hart poetically marvels at how Christ uses truth "in a world where power, riches, and violence seduce hearts and compel assent, he persuades and prevails not as a tyrant, an armed assailant, or a man of wealth, but simply as a teacher of God and his love.... Christ is a persuasion, a form of evoking desire."[29] God is truth, yet because we do not possess God, we cannot own or fully grasp the truth. Rather we may say that as humans we operate by many truths, and for those we may deem worthy and authentic, they offer glimpses of God.

Imagination and Transformation

From a theopoetic viewpoint, imagination is essential for preaching. Paul Ricoeur defines imagination as "the power of giving form to human experience or... the power of redescribing reality."[30] When preachers interpret a biblical text for today, they redescribe reality and thereby point to new realities. Imagination used to be conceived as opposed to reason, and like the emotions, it was wild and untrustworthy. Nowadays, imagination is understood not as false, but as an aide in perceiving truth. Imagination allows us to project into the future the effects of actions and thereby to avoid danger. Imagination runs the metaphor store, and theology and theopoetry cannot do their tasks without coming to shop.

Imagination allows preachers to look on a situation of injustice and to picture what it might look like were the realm of God not temporarily thwarted. It has the potential to take evil seriously through vivid description and narrative. Imagination finds in every act of goodness an affirmation of the resurrection and in every moment seeks an in-breaking of the end times, the future present, when Christ will come again. Imagination offers dreams, false to some, but for those who seek relief from the tyranny at the foot of the cross, they offer the deep consolation and truth of experienced faith and transformed lives in Easter light.

Part of the reason truth is transformative in preaching is that imagination is prophetic: By dreaming what God wants, the preacher opens the possibility of hearers reaching it. As the angel Gabriel announced to Mary, "Nothing is impossible for God" (Luke 1:37). Without dreams that things might be different, there is little hope of change. Imagination supplies such dreams with the aid of the Spirit. Imagination takes the first steps toward change and the One who is all truth confirms it.

Literary critic Hayden White said the old distinction between history as real and imagination as fiction now needs to be rethought. History and imagination "overlap, resemble, or correspond with each other."[31] Viewers of the popular BBC production *Downton Abbey* gain an authentic sense of the World War I period, though the show is fiction. Daniel Aaron laments that "scientific historians" have taken over history with "the no-nonsense monograph, conceived by specialists for other specialists and stripped of pageantry, descriptive set pieces, dramatic confrontations, and authorial reflections."[32] As a result some writers "have begun to smudge the boundary line between history and fiction, to blend them, and to assert that fictional history might be 'truer' than recorded history."[33] The teeter-totter of history and the future has shifted: the past used to weigh more. Now the future has more weight; we already have glimpses of it in developing technology. Popular "historical" films are recognized as current interpretations of the past, which shifts the past even more into the present. Preachers are advised to portray the biblical events in present tense, not just to make the prose more vital, but also to avoid sounding like history.

Imagination and truth are of particular relevance for preachers dealing with the Bible. The preacher is charged with making the text sound not like math, cut and dried, but real life, and that involves in effect making a movie of the text. This is not a process of making things up out of nothing or of distorting what the text says, but it is painting the picture with details authentic to the time and period, creating as much of the original lived context as possible. The wedding at Cana (John 2:1-12) is filled with smells of wine and cooking food, though the text does not detail them. Stories about the contemporary world also need to come alive. Authenticity is an issue: The preacher must be seen to care about the people portrayed, and must believe what is said.

Critic Zhang Longxi notes, "The past cannot be fully present in the historical account."[34] He speaks against confusing history with truth, words worth pondering by preachers too immersed in historical criticism. "Historical grounding turns out to be nothing more than constructing a context for a literary text out of other historical accounts, and the obvious circularity of such textual construction makes it difficult to substantiate any claim to historical truth or authenticity."[35] He concludes, "Hence, truth is what is best imagined, and the novelist is obviously better qualified than the historian to locate and reattach invisible historical links."[36] The same might be said of preachers. When we create movies of biblical texts with our words, using poetry, we may be closer to representing the historical events than if we describe them in the dry and often dehumanized manner of much history.

Theopoetics and Reconstruction

Deconstruction uses binary poles. What is the pole to deconstruction itself that prevents it from totalitarian claims? How may preachers understand their efforts to produce positive meaning? Is there something like literary reconstruction (not a very poetic term) to balance deconstruction (even worse)? There needs to be because a good part of the preacher's task is to participate in Christ's own activity of recreating, making all things new.

Some years ago I wrote of S. T. Coleridge's idea of imagination that he defined as the "juxtaposition" or "reconciliation of opposites."[37] My high school physics class helped me understand him, for there we had a hand-crank generator from an old telephone. The generator had two wires, one from the positive pole and one from the negative. If someone cranked the generator we saw something remarkable. If the wires were held about six inches apart, a spark of electricity like lightning jumped the gap from the positive wire to the negative. If the wires were too far apart, there was no spark; the electrical charge was dissipated to the air. If the wires touched there was again no spark; the current flowed through the wires.

Imagination brings ideas together in a manner similar to those two wires. A spark of new meaning is created between them. The metaphor "love is a red rose" brings love and a red rose together and a third identity is produced, and that third identity is the meaning of the metaphor. Love is tender like a rose, needs much care, is associated with the heart and the color red, and is often beautiful. Metaphors have a no and a yes. No, love is not a flower, it is an emotion, but the yes of new meaning is finally stronger than the no. Coleridge said that imagination is "the reconciliation of opposites": he meant that it harnesses the creative energy between the two, not that the energy between them is neutralized or removed.

Coleridge's revolutionary insight was that poetry creates new meaning by linking two ideas that might not otherwise be connected. The ideas must have some legitimate connection or there will be no spark. For example, there is nothing in common between love and a terrorist, therefore "love is a terrorist" does not work. On the other hand, ideas that are too similar ("love is a kiss") may have no spark. They are ho-hum. Language lives and dies. Eventually all metaphors lose their spark and return to the land of math, as we see, for instance, with "the leg of a table," which is now understood literally.

Perhaps physics and wires are not your thing. Here is an analogy to relationships: In earlier notions of marriage, the woman was expected to lose her identity and take on that of her husband. They became so similar there was little spark of difference. Today if people marry and retain their own identities, there is a spark; it is the third identity that they make when they are together as a couple.

Metaphor is not just a frill or decoration, as it was in Aristotelian and modernist thinking. Metaphor is how language works and is one major way humans think. When preachers bring two things into a tensive relationship, as long as there is something in common between them, creative energy is generated and new meaning is possible.

Metaphor is how language works and is one major way humans think.

Coleridge was postmodern yet ahead of his time. Scholars seem not to have noticed how Coleridge's ideas of imagination and contemporary ideas of deconstruction mirror each other. Deconstruction mostly takes apart meaning, while imagination generates it. Both disrupt the status quo: Deconstruction undermines existing realities while imagination generates new ones. Both are historical reactions against the Enlightenment's overemphasis on reason and logic. Both function using poles in language: With deconstruction, the poles are binary opposites. With imagination, the poles are individual words or images with their own separate identities yet that have some link. Both demonstrate Ricoeur's yes and no: In deconstruction, the yes (to the equal value of the binary poles) is overcome by a louder no (to the hierarchy of binary terms employed by the speaker). In Coleridge's imagination, by contrast, the no (to the equality of the poles) is overcome by the louder yes (to the new meaning of the metaphor). In both, meaning is eventful, fleeting. All of this is to say that deconstruction is not the only postmodern option for preachers and they need not associate postmodernity with mainly tearing things apart. Some postmodern notions of language are highly creative and dedicated to producing beautiful, good, new meanings and truths.

Six Practices for Faithful Imagination

Imagination may in part be an innate creative ability but it is also something that can be learned by preachers through training. If a sermon you are working on seems flat and in need of creativity, here are six exercises to try using imagination:

(1) Juxtapose Ideas, Stories, Emotions, or Images

Check to see if you might harness any of the below pairings to create interest:

- Trouble and grace, particularly as an overall tension as the sermon moves from one to the other.
- A biblical text and a contemporary situation that is similar or contrasting. Barbara Brown Taylor once told the story of a woman with serious health issues and then read from Isaiah these words that seemed to have extra power: "Strengthen the weak hands, / and make firm the feeble knees. / Say to those who are of a fearful heart, / 'Be strong, do not fear!'" (Isa 35:3-4 NRSV). You might tell the biblical story of the prodigal, and then tell the story of a teenage runaway today.
- A biblical text and other biblical passages related by image, words, or opposing perspectives. Jonah was swallowed by a whale and Jesus was swallowed by death.

- Two contemporary stories showing contrasting impact of the same words. Two people walk by a woman with a sandwich board on which is written the word *repent.* One contemplates it and decides there is nothing to change; another uses it as the occasion to stop smoking.
- Two different personalities, one who operates by head and the other by heart or one who is generous and the other who is not.
- A child's perspective and an adult's.
- Lament and celebration.[38]

(2) Present "Truth" Often in Contrapuntal Ways

James M. Childs is sensitive to controversies concerning truth these days, and the danger of distorting truth by asserting it too flatly. For example, he advises preachers against asking in a sermon if the virgin birth is true, or if the resurrection is true, when skepticism seems so rampant. Instead he suggests asking, "What if it is true?" and in so doing allow other options.[39] It keeps the conversation open. It also invites preachers to ask, "What if it's not true?"—yet a further contrapuntal route of exploration. Listeners are more likely to claim what is true for themselves when truth is presented with its counterpoints. Given our earlier discussion about truth as an experience of the living God, we might offer an alternative to Child's questions: "What if it is God's nature to . . . ?" and "What if it is God's nature not to . . . ?"

(3) Make Movies

A typical problem for many new preachers is that they are too much into their heads. They leave seminary and realize that most of their formal training was for essay writing, not dynamic oral communication. They deal too much in abstractions and propositions and not enough in the concrete language and imagery of oral culture. Preachers schooled to write essays can be captivated by their own abstract thoughts, but for many people in the congregation abstract thoughts may be boring. These preachers could be encouraged to get out of their heads and into their feelings, and out of the prose of faith and into poetry.

One simple way to add creativity to a sermon is to picture in words what one talks about. Visualize your text, perhaps through praying it, seeing each detail verse by verse, and being there. Without going into much descriptive detail, make a movie of the text. Moviemakers have to make decisions about things that are not in the biblical text or the commentaries, like what was the weather like, what were the people wearing, what sounds can be heard, what smells can be smelled? Just a few details are needed, not long passages of description. Keep the main emphasis on action, on people doing things. Give a few words for key characters to say, ideally from the text itself. Stay out of their heads as much as possible, in the way that movies communicate through a characters gestures, movements, words, and emotions. The more lifelike the picture, the easier it is for the listener to understand, and the more interesting and imaginative the sermon experience.

(4) Use Prophetic Visioning

Do not paint in detail the worst situation you mention in your sermon: Details of violence and evil can be too powerful and too hard to counter. Mention bad events and name the issues but do not completely take us there. By contrast, visualize or imagine later in your sermon a similar scene when God's love reigns. In the book *Spiritual Leadership,* author Henry Blackaby argues that secular leaders cast a vision and then get people to buy in. By contrast, spiritual leaders seek the vision God wants for the congregation and reveal it.[40] A former student writes that seeking God's vision has changed her approach to preaching. In her preparation each week she now prays for the vision that God has for the community. We can use prophetic visioning to dream, for instance, what effect we would have on peace if we could give even a portion of the defense budget to building and funding schools in Third World countries. Or we could dream about how neighborhoods could be more electronically linked, so we could better take care of one another. Or we could dream about how anti-bullying programs could be better implemented in local schools. There is no limit to dreaming what God wants.

(5) Imagine Experiences of Encounter with Christ

A common way for preachers to appeal to truth is to pull a statement out as a kind of proof for an argument, like "We know things will be okay because Jesus is raised from the dead" or "We know that God knows our pain because God's Son died on the cross." Such statements may be accurate and effective for the faithful, but for those who struggle with faith, they may not work. They are propositions disconnected from present life experience. They are believe-it-or-not, or head-on truth. It can be better to tell the truth slant, to angle it through experience. For example, help people identify that they have experienced Jesus raised from the dead in their own lives: like when they were lost and were found, or without hope and received hope; or when they were in mourning and were comforted, or in prayer. Imagination converts propositional truths into lived experience.

(6) Honor the Mystery: Acknowledge What Has No Answer

Sometimes it takes imagination to know what should not be said to avoid turning the poetry of faith into math, or to use Paul's language, turning the Spirit into the letter, "for the letter kills, but the Spirit gives life" (2 Cor 3:6 NRSV). David Brooks wrote powerfully of the lessons learned by the Woodiwiesse family in dealing with two separate tragedies in their lives: "[They] warned against those who would overinterpret, and try to make sense of the inexplicable. Even devout Christians, as the Woodiwisses are, should worry about taking theology beyond its limits. Theology is a grounding in ultimate hope, not a formula book to explain away each individual event."[41] The suggestion is to recognize disappointment with God, or the seeming absence of God, or doubt about God, without trying to make things all better.

Preachers who have felt threatened by postmodernity may have felt particularly threatened by its critique of truth and metanarratives. In this chapter we have shown that modern notion of fixed, objective, or universal truth, in fact, have attractive postmodern alternatives. These alternatives arise out of an understanding that truth is relational, and the best relational understandings are revealed in a relationship with God. Indeed, truth is the character of God. In the next chapter we ask if truth is fully served, (1) if the pulpit does not include in its agenda the importance of civil discourse and (2) if the pattern and setting of traditional worship does not offer choices. We do this not necessarily to advocate a particular change in how we conceive of worship, but at least to raise concerns that may be in the minds of many people not attending church, and to further a conversation relevant to our postmodern age.

Chapter Eight
Truth and Worship (Homiletics)

A common modernist assumption that many Christians continue to hold is that truth is best served when congregations have a common mind, and that worship is one-size-fits-all. Unity, the argument goes, means common understanding, like minds and interests. This way of thinking about unity is one reason postmodernity is suspicious of it: It demands conformity. It imposes standards on those who are different with expectations that they measure up. Worship in many churches is like it or leave it. Postmodernity, by contrast, welcomes diversity. Many contemporary writers eschew unity, as though the modern understanding of it is the only one possible. Postmodern ideas can provide alternative ways of thinking about worship that may appeal to some people who currently have no interest in church. Postmodern thought also suggests that truth is not best served when people conceive of it along party lines or when competing understandings of truth are suppressed.

David Lose tells a disturbing story of a couple who had a conversation with their children about whether to continue attending their local church. They found themselves overextended in terms of work, social, and school commitments and had a family consultation:

> After an hour and a half of conversation, they came to their decisions. And church was one of the things they had decided to *stop* doing. Girl Scouts remained, but church was out. "It's just not that meaningful," the man explained. "We go each week and finally realized we're not getting anything out of it. It's hard to believe I'm saying this," he continued. "Our parents took us; and once we had kids we took them, too. But it just doesn't connect with the rest of our lives. So we're done."[1]

This story is sufficiently common it would seem, from dwindling church memberships, to require a creative response from churches.

To that end, we will begin here by exploring if the preaching might model and encourage better truth making by encouraging civil discourse. We will then consider how the worship context of preaching might affect people's openness to truth, how sermon form might point to truth, and consider if worship in some settings needs an overhaul.

Truth and Civil Discourse

At the end of a long day of summer school class, a D. Min. student from the oil patch where the oil industry is a key employer responded to another's sermon, "In my congregation, I cannot even mention energy conservation." The energy level of the class suddenly rose like oil at a wellhead, as if this preacher's confession had tapped into each person's own experience. Each had a story to tell about what one called the "pulpit trap door": Say the wrong thing and the pulpit floor will fall away, and the preacher's job with it. Such is the polarized nature of much discourse today, which raises an important question about truth for the pulpit. In the current social climate, can preachers address serious social issues in meaningful ways or are they limited to the dominant political party line? Might churches have a role in fostering civic discourse and what might that look like in preaching? Can preaching be an instrument to equip listeners better to engage neighbors in conversation? Might civil discourse be a new form of evangelism? There are dangers and possibilities in this proposal.

A Polarized Society

With all of the social media, one might expect that this would be an age in which open discussion flourishes. Ironically, however, in the midst of increased cultural diversity and interconnectivity, society is increasingly polarized, civic involvement is on the wane among youth, volunteerism is down, and civil discourse is lacking. Mass media once had something of a unifying influence on culture and now is replaced by what Don Tapscott calls "molecular media." People "can listen to, read, or watch the views they support or hold. That means there is a real danger of balkanization in our society—we all may end up in self-reinforcing echo chambers where all we hear is our own point of view."[2]

Sharon Crowley, whose main interest is civic discourse, sees the division in American culture to be between Christian fundamentalism and liberalism, and each has its own densely articulated view of what citizenship requires.[3] Other scholars see the polarization to be between those with middle-to-high incomes and those with lower income and no benefits.[4] The Pew Research Center finds that between 2005 and 2009, inflation-adjusted wealth fell for white households by 16 percent; for African American, 53 percent; and for Hispanic, 66 percent; and the wealth gap between white and African American households is now 20 to 1, up from 7 to 1 in 1995.[5] Thomas Bender bemoans a "thinning" of American culture that has a diminished interplay between social life and politics.[6]

Polarized Truth

Local churches commonly have as hard a time as the rest of society in discussing controversial issues and hearing contrary opinions. Society is litigious and often adversarial. Most people are uncomfortable with conflict and are not trained to handle it well. Differences of opinion often are taken personally and can cause anger and lingering resentment. Acquaintances, colleagues, and even family avoid issues of difference lest relationships be strained or irreparably harmed.

The life of the church is negatively affected by its own difficulty to talk in open and civil ways about many issues, including the growing national and global disparity between rich and poor, environmental degradation, energy use, climate change, racism, issues of gender and sexuality, diversity, bioethics, fresh water, war, and the list goes on. Many of these issues are not discussed in pulpits because they are seen as too divisive. Congregations have discovered how quickly discussions, for instance, about sexuality become uncivil, disagreements become personal, and people threaten to leave. If the ability of pulpits to discuss important ethical matters is compromised, so too is the church's ability to act in meaningful ways on key issues.

What alternatives are there? Some churches go silent on social issues, and indeed many people would prefer to limit church talk to sin and salvation. Others argue that the church's past silence on key issues like the Holocaust, sexism, and racism are lasting stains upon its conscience. Churches can become island communities of like-minded folks making moral pronouncements that merely reinforce that group's positions. Another possibility is that the church might adopt as part of its mission the promotion of civil discourse and compassion for all, and in so doing show leadership to society. For this to happen, civil discourse might need to be part of the intentional agenda of preaching.

Civil Discourse as a Way to Seek Truth

Civil discourse is needed because of competing understandings of truth. Kenneth J. Gergen describes civil discourse as an act of being modest, respectful of the other's moral worth and judgment, and avoiding antagonism and excessive argumentation; in modernist terms, it is the "language of dispassionate objectivity."[7] Civil discourse is humble, constructive, and builds on what is held in common. Civil discourse overlaps with public discourse, which is public conversation about public issues, as in town hall meetings.

In theory, at least, the church is well situated to model civil discourse for society. Preaching often engages it simply by discussing difficult issues in balanced ways and by preachers participating in civic social policies, social outreach, ecumenical and interfaith dialogue, and other ways. Those involved are church leaders. Little is done to equip congregational members for civil discourse inside and outside the congregation. Martin Marty quipped that, "people who are good at being civil often lack strong convictions and people who have strong convictions often lack civility."[8] Civil discourse might become at least a frequent reference point of sermons.

Little is done to equip congregational members for civil discourse inside and outside the congregation.

Richard J. Mouw, a long-time advocate for the importance of Christian civility, is quick to note, "Not that civil decency is the be-all and end-all of life. We will not solve all our problems simply by becoming more civil people. There are times when it is appropriate to manifest some very uncivil feelings. 'Passionate intensity' is not always out of place. If I am going to be a more civil person, it cannot be because I have learned to ignore my convictions."[9] Mouw calls for combining a civil outlook with "passionate intensity" or "convicted civility."[10] "I believe that being civil is a way of becoming more like what God intends us to be."[11] Civil discourse will find ways for everyone to have a voice and to be respectful of someone's silence.

Writers in homiletics have spoken on issues relating to civil discourse. John McClure has argued for many years the empowering nature of consultative and collaborative leadership,[12] and he encouraged a round table approach to the sermon by having representative focus groups meet with the preacher to reflect on the upcoming sermon.[13] He wants to "reconnect the gospel message with the public realm."[14] Lucy Rose encouraged a round table approach by having representative members of the congregation preach.[15] Brian Blount[16] and Justo González call for the church to be intentionally multicultural in congregational worship. As González says, "not simply because our society is multicultural, but because the future from which God is calling us is multicultural."[17] Ron Allen has advised how to preach on controversial issues so that various perspectives are honored, even though one position may be recommended.[18] Robert Reid has developed a model for public speech on matters of values dispute: It involves being willing to be deeply respectful of the argument of the other, listening carefully, framing both positions well, and only then making an argument for why the society you want to live in is best served by one rather than the other position.[19]

What models are there for civil discourse? Wayne Booth believes that one can stand one's ground within a tradition of belief and still share things in common with those with whom one does not agree.[20] Karen and Sonja Foss argue that persuasion and argument has no further place of pride in communication theory (seeking to move the center to dialogue). They advocate an invitational dialogue that is informative on controversial issues yet that is respectful by not taking a side.[21] A good part of any model needs to be establishing the right setting for such a dialogue. More needs to be done in terms of the church interacting with culture. O. Wesley Allen suggests that if theological talk is to have a meaningful role in postmodern society,

> it will require more than bringing conversation into worship. It will also require more than having broader and more frequent conversations about sermons or having preachers step out of high pulpits and stand at floor level to offer conversational sermons. There needs to be more conscious, theologically oriented conversation throughout the congregation—more circles of conversation in which church talk seriously engages all of the other conversations going on in our culture as people try to make meaning in a relative yet global context.[22]

Resistance to Civil Discourse

Might some forms of civil discourse compromise Christian identity? Were a church to host town or church hall meetings, people would speak contrary to positions held by the church. The three-year Penn National Commission on Society, Culture, and Community (1996–1999) explored the state of public discourse and public behavior in the United States. Among other conclusions, it said that if polarization in public discourse is to be overcome there must be a willingness not only to express strongly held positions but also a willingness to have them modified.[23] Some people say that people who strictly adhere to religious or political systems have less ability to compromise or be modified than those who do not, thus civil discourse can be problematic.

What standards or principles might guide civil discourse? At a basic level, John McClure held up the Bible as the standard for the roundtable discussions.[24] Lenora Tubbs Tisdale, writing on worship wars in the church, held up theological "channel markers" to prevent discussions from running aground.[25] The gospel is a worthy standard, but as Brian Blount notes, the gospel in fact heightens cultural tensions because Jesus insists that all people are God's people and they need to be heard.[26] Pablo A. Jiménez argues that in contrast to colonial mission preaching, postcolonial preaching needs to avoid legitimizing "Anglo-European hegemony, focusing on personal salvation and morality . . . largely unaware of its social, economic, and political role."[27] Luke Powery says that postcolonial interpretation "proclaims the need for justice at all levels of society, condemning spirituality that is only concerned with personal piety and oblivious to the sociopolitical implications of religion."[28]

The complexity of these kinds of issues might speak against civil discourse, yet because these issues run so deep, they are part of the reason for it. One of the best reasons for civil discourse is to follow God's will and to contribute to a world that is less polarized, less prone to hatred and violence. Civil discourse is a willingness to dialogue in a common search for truth without sacrificing identity and beliefs and without believing that one possesses all truth. If the church does more to sponsor civil discourse as a means of outreach, formats could be created to encourage it.

Truth and Worship

Recent notions of truth imply several changes may be needed in the church of tomorrow. They may be briefly listed as questions:

(1) Can the church of tomorrow be more invitational and open to diversity? Uniformity or conformity in many places is now rejected as a social project. Pluralism is valued as is acceptance of diversity, among youth in particular.

(2) Can the church seek its unity not in static fashion in formulations of beliefs, but in daily reliance upon the Spirit? Communities of sameness might then become communities of difference centered in Christ.

(3) Can the church be a place where differences are welcomed, not merely tolerated? An open and invitational congregation might find community in what the Spirit does to hold the community together.

(4) Can the church be less controlling of the packaging, supply, and delivery of its message? The latest generations want to be more in control of their own learning, finding their own way, and discovering at their own pace. They want the freedom to make mistakes.

(5) Can churches allow for less denominational emphasis? The latest generations are not much interested in historical division; they are interested in links with other Christians, and often with people of other faiths.

(6) Can churches provide opportunities for different paths and styles of learning? Howard Gardner, Professor of Cognition and Education at Harvard, identifies seven kinds of intelligence: linguistic, musical, logical, spatial, kinesthetic, interpersonal, and intrapersonal (awareness of self).[29] Each has implications for teaching.

(7) Can the church shift its teaching more in the direction of practices and experience? People today seem more interested in practices and experience than beliefs on their own. New attention can be devoted to support individuals in their own learning processes, often by trial and error and mixing and matching.

One Size Does Not Fit All

Postmodernity is suspicious of unity, and would challenge the modernist assumption that in worship one size fits all. What is poetry to some in worship is not poetry to others, and what is math to some is poetry to others. Books abound on liturgy and alternative worship. Recently, Bryan D. Spynks wrote *Worship Mall,*[30] in which he looks at the emergent church movement, megachurches, liquid worship (where for part of the service people independently visit one or two various stations), seeker services, multisensory services, Celtic options, and post-Vatican II liturgies. Some of these practices are experimental but they all seek to contribute to the overall worship experience. Of course, even if preachers were to stand on their heads and juggle flaming torches on the pulpit, there is no guarantee it would attract those indifferent to the church.

Does traditional worship not already provide for different interests? Some might say yes because of the different parts of the service. In 1960, the Church of the Savior in Washington, DC, established an outreach ministry to be in dialogue with the world and offer different kinds of services throughout the week. Many people seeking spiritual direction want interpersonal connection and spiritual growth through conversations and relationships. They may turn to alternative forms of spiritual community (e.g., house churches, religious programs, intentional communities, workplace ministries, church online, or attending Christian concerts). As one researcher pointedly says, for many people, "Repeating the same weekly routines in religious events is increasingly deemed anachronistic, stifling and irrelevant. Rigidity of belief—which includes the notion that there are absolute moral and spiritual truths—[is] perceived by a large (and growing) share of young people to be evidence of closed-mindedness."[31]

Is it possible that the worship service as it is currently conceived is a barrier to some people in their pursuit of truth? Jesus said, "The Sabbath was created for humans; humans weren't created for the Sabbath" (Mark 2:27), and that might apply to the worship hour as well. What further options are there?

Is it possible that the worship service as it is currently conceived is a barrier to some people in their pursuit of truth?

We tend to think of worship as the worship service. Our ancestors understood worship as everything we do in life, the dedication of our entire lives to God in thanksgiving and praise. Worship in this sense is how one uses one's gifts and who or what one chooses to honor; it is the giving of thanks to God in all of life. I like this broadened definition because it speaks of a worship that knows no boundaries. It is what Jesus spoke about when he told followers to love God with all your heart, being, mind, and strength

(Mark 12:30). This is unconfined worship. It knows no limits and puts up no barriers. Such worship is remarkably inclusive, hospitable to all. It lacks one thing—community.

Dreaming about New Worship Models for Truth Seeking

Here I simply dream about an alternate way to conceive of preaching and worship, not because I think we should abandon current practices, nor to advocate a new model, but mainly as a way to challenge existing assumptions. People today want choice; they want to be in control of their own learning with the freedom of trial and error, and they want practical outcomes.

I imagine something that might be called modular worship, where the whole of Sunday morning (or some other time block) is dedicated to worship. Instead of one-size-fits-all, in this model there are many options.[32] Individuals design their own experience—they determine their own order of service. The morning is divided into a number of time periods, fifteen to thirty minutes long. Each period ideally might have more than one module operating at the same time in order to provide some choice. The total number of module offerings would depend on available space, leadership resources, and the size of the congregation. Individuals choose which modules to attend and devise their own order of worship according to their interests. They attend for all of the morning or just drop in, as their schedules permit.

Modules are of three types: praise, mission, and community. Praise modules are organized around elements of the worship service: One module would be devoted to readings from the Bible, perhaps with discussion; another would focus on prayer; and another would offer music by the choir, a musician, as hymns, or whatever. Because of the importance of the Word, the sermon is a stand-alone module, intended for the whole community, perhaps even children.[33] On occasion, when the preacher is required to lead another module, a video sermon might be played.

Mission modules are based on the activities of the church that help it fulfill its mission, including Sunday school classes, sermon discussion, pre-marriage sessions, food bank, and the like. A few slots on the timetable, perhaps early in the morning, are reserved for short meetings that might otherwise take place during the week, thus making good use of members' time.

Community modules in particular allow for diversity and dialogue with the world. Their purpose is (a) to honor and showcase the God-given gifts of people within the church and larger community, and to uphold those gifts within the context of worship, (b) to introduce the congregation to resource people in the community they might not otherwise meet, (c) to introduce people to the church who might not otherwise come, and (d) to provide the kind of experience a community center might provide, with Christ at its center. Artists could speak about their art; immigrants could speak about their issues; financial experts could offer basic financial management; homemakers would teach home management skills; young people could speak about their schools; food banks would talk about urban gardening, and so on. Getting men to church is sometimes difficult,[34] thus community modules might be devoted to special projects that might appeal particularly but not exclusively to men, like Habitat for Humanity—whatever is needed in the church or community.

In this model, a café operates throughout the morning. Anyone not wanting to attend a module session might go to the café, either to chat over coffee or to help prepare a lunch. One of the reasons for church is community, people talking, and in this model of worship conversations happen in modules, between modules, and over a meal. The rite of Holy Communion would be part of the lunch, akin to the practice in 1 Corinthians 11:17-34. In our expanded definition of worship, the entire morning would be considered the worship service, an offering to God.

What we have here is a sketch, but even at that, modular worship stands as a symbol of possible changes in some churches in the future. It is intended here not as an argument against traditional worship services, but rather as a way to start conversations, challenge assumptions, and raise questions about worship as a traditional fixed form, particularly about the adequacy of discipleship formation provided by a single worship hour. It affirms that Christians are called to worship with their whole lives, that biblical preaching is vital to church life, and that worship leads to faith and service. Finally, it proposes that the church can be united under Christ even with differences, that the church can be community to more than believers, that true community is based on unconditional love for all, and that people can come to Christ through many paths.

Modular worship has implications for preaching. The preacher, in addition to pastoral duties, assumes more of a teaching/preaching role as theologian-in-residence. Rather than being CEO or coordinator of modules, an administrative role that others in the community could fill, the preacher would be a pastor and a theological resource to the modules. Moreover, the preacher as theologian-in-residence might be intentional about offering appropriate theopoetic reflection in any setting: a posted thought for the day, a pastoral word to an individual parishioner, a comment in a blog, a reflection offered at the beginning of a meeting. Each of these could be considered as a sermon, or at least as sermon elements of what might be a modular sermon on Sunday.

Here is an example of a particularly fine short "sermon" in a weekly blog by a minister to his church:

> Dear Friends,
>
> Yesterday was one of those days where nothing seemed to be going right. It started with the death of one of our Life Deacons, Eldred Gooding. Beyond that there were a number of things, mostly little, that just didn't go as hoped. Then towards the end of the day I had a message concerning a church member in the hospital whose day wasn't going so well either. I left a meeting early and arrived at the hospital a little after visiting hours had come to an end. The lights were low and the halls were quiet.
>
> It was good to just sit and pray at the end of the day with someone whose faith is deep and rich. On leaving the hospital room a man introduced himself as the husband of the woman in the next bed. He had heard me read the scriptures and pray and asked if I was a pastor. It turned out he and his wife were a long ways from their northern Ontario home and missing the presence of their own pastor. Two months ago his wife was diagnosed with a rare disease and the two have been fighting an uphill battle in our city ever since.
>
> In a moment we turned back into the same room and I read again the scriptures and offered prayers for a woman who seemed very sick. "Do you have a favorite scripture I can read for you?" I asked. She wasn't the first person to suggest Psalm 139, and so as I read I couldn't help but think of some dear folk now in Glory who clung to those same beautiful words of the God who is "too lofty for me to attain," and yet who, "knit me together in my mother's womb," and in whom we are "fearfully and wonderfully made." Psalm 139 is a song in praise of God, who is always with us and sees us through and beyond.
>
> As two people of faith sharing a hospital room put their hope in God, I went from the room so blessed that looking back on the day, I literally couldn't remember what had been bothering me before I entered the room. I like to think I visit the sick to bring them hope and faith and encouragement, but so often it is their hope and faith that strengthens me.
>
> Please say a prayer today for Catherine from Northern Ontario and for Julie in the adjacent bed. Pray too for the family of Eldred Gooding. And I am sure I don't need to remind you to keep praying for the people of Moore,

Oklahoma. I don't know what today will bring, but I know God is with us and will see us through.

Grace and Peace,
The Rev. Dr. J. Peter Holmes[35]

Most preachers have something of a scrapyard of sermon parts that they go to when a sermon needs a fender, a steering wheel, or shock absorbers. I can imagine that if the preacher were to be more of a theopoet-in-residence there would be several short reflections written each week for different purposes. We spoke earlier of sermons composed as bricolage and of rhizomatic form. It would be fun to imagine a weekly sermon practice that might pull several of these intentional pieces together around the biblical text for the week.

Chapter Nine

Truth as Pentecost Transformation (Practice)

In this chapter we return mainly to theopoetic expression and the third grand moment of gospel celebration in the church year, namely Pentecost. We spoke of Christmas as beginnings of faith and of Easter as central content of faith. Now at the end of this project we speak of endings, ending the sermon in hope, the gift of the Holy Spirit accompanying us until the end of time, and of endings in Christ as new beginnings. In other words, we speak of the power of truth to transformed lives in the present and for the future.

Some denominations do not talk a lot about the Holy Spirit and transformation. Too much of what some people call the Spirit can be off-putting, like speaking in tongues, snake handling, and drinking poison (Mark 16:17-18). At the same time, many of us with European heritage would love to worship in a congregation that rocks and moves like some African American ones, filled with energy and rhythm that makes one want to dance; you leave feeling pumped up not weighed down, empowered by the "Spirit of truth" (John 14:17; 16:13) for ministry during the week. Yet what a wonderful experience it can be in any worship when our imaginations are stretched to conceive of the Holy Spirit acting in our lives, here, gathering and shaping us as a community of Christ, and there, serving the world with transforming power. Perceiving by imagination, we glimpse what is true, real, authentic, beautiful, and good.

The National Hockey League Calgary Flames, formerly the Atlanta Flames, have not burned down the ice sufficiently to win the Stanley Cup more than once, in 1989. By contrast, in the Bible, flames that do not burn are often the mark of the Holy Spirit. Isaiah said, "The light of Israel will become a fire, / its holy one a flame" (10:17). The flames of the burning bush that Moses sees do not consume the bush or wither its leaves (Exod 3:2) and the live coal that touches Isaiah's lips and cleanses him does not sear his lips (Isa 6:6-7). In the fiery furnace, Shadrach, Meshach, and Abednego are found unbound, walking, and unhurt with a fourth person of divine appearance (Dan 3:25), whom many Christians through history have identified as Christ. John the Baptist's promises that Jesus will baptize "with the Holy Spirit and fire" (Luke 3:16) and, of course, tongues of fire rest upon the disciples at Pentecost (Acts 2:3).

Imagining the First Pentecost

Let us assume that today is the first Pentecost. Many times we may have walked in the early morning along these narrow cobbled streets of Old Jerusalem, past children playing and sleeping dogs, Roman soldiers on horseback and adults coming back from the market. Other followers of Jesus, about 120, are already singing hymns as we wash our feet in the atrium, and find a seat on the floor. The singing is simple, and then Peter and Mary the mother of Jesus stand and speak. They remember Jesus, his sayings, his stories, his deeds, his promise to send his Spirit. They speak with muted expression. Math is at the door with its pointed questions for believers: "What is truth? Is anything is to be believed?" It is hard to rise to poetry if as a community you may question whether your experience was even true. It has been ten days since Jesus's ascension, ten long days of waiting.

The day is dark but suddenly the sky is blue. Light as bright as the sun suddenly floods the room along with the sound of a violent wind, but the air is still. At just the sound, the women clasp their shawls and reach for the hands of their children. Fire seems to dance on each person like reflected sunlight off a lake, yet there is no lake. Everyone starts to talk at once in each other's language. Not babble—it is more like sweet music with true harmonies come down from heaven; your own native language seems spoken by all. We make sense of it, because we hear English. If you come from the deep South, you hear everyone speaking with a southern drawl, and Canadians hear folks say *out* and *about* and *schedule* the way John Wesley intended. It is like truth whooshed into that room, deep peace, abiding love, and overflowing joy. It is a good thing.

But it may not seem like a good thing if you are on the outside looking in, if you are one of the Jerusalem neighbors gathered to find out what all the commotion was about. No matter what hour, if people are having a party and you are not invited, if you are an onlooker, if it looks like people are having a good time and you are having a bad day, it is not always a positive experience.

Worship that Rocks

Hartford Memorial Baptist Church is an African American church in Detroit formerly pastored by Charles G. Adams. They have six choirs of sixty. When their soloists open their mouths, the gates of heaven seem to open. The choirs have that two-step that gets the whole front of the church rocking with the music. Adams himself would catch fire in the pulpit, "The new right, is nothing but the old wrong." After church the people are all fired up, welcoming and speaking about their faith. You go once to Hartford Baptist and you come away all fired up yourself. You go twice and you are reliving the experience. But you go three times and you are starting to think about how your own church may not measure up. In some of our churches the choir is so still they've hired a nurse to check pulses. The choir director has members smile every fifteen minutes, just to see if they are alive. Lord knows, some of our preaching is more sad, bad, and mad than glad; folks in the pews take out their cellular phones to call home during the sermon just to feel better. People can get used to thinking that truth is only depressing, but that in itself is a lie.

Why is it that some churches seem to have so much of the Holy Spirit and some so little? Peter preaches on Joel. If God really has poured out God's Spirit upon all flesh, why doesn't my son or your daughter even go to church, much less prophesy? Why are some church schools down more than 90 percent since 1964? Oh, if God really has poured out God's Spirit on all flesh, why is it that some people have good marriages while others break up; why do some people have jobs while others don't even have the education and training to find work; why are some nations so wealthy while entire peoples worry whether food will come tomorrow? You can have too much of a good thing, more than your share. A few times visiting the first Pentecost can leave us sorely troubled by the inequities and iniquities of life. We may not want to party and join in all the poetry. We might prefer to be among the gathering crowd outside, figuring out why things don't add up and all things aren't equal, casting our lot instead with those who dismiss the celebrations as early drunkenness and potent wine.

Surely we are not the first to note the iniquities and inequities of life. One might look at the whole Christian story and say God noted them well in coming in Christ, and noted also we were no match for them, no match for evil. Jesus eventually knew our weakness all too well and he laid down his life because we were no match for the trouble in us and around us. One for many; the math did not work.

Jesus's followers knew their own utter helplessness after Jesus left them. For days they waited to be given direction and empowerment by the Holy Spirit. Jesus was right; without him, they could do nothing (John 15:5). They lived only on a promise and a prayer. He had promised to send his Spirit to them. Ten days of spiritual drought might not seem like a long time, but if you don't know what is true or what to believe, if you feel helpless, if nothing seems to work, it can seem like an eternity. Grief and common memory bind Jesus's followers one to another, not strength. They meditate on the beautiful names of the Holy Spirit Jesus promised would descend on them: Advocate, Comforter, Counsellor, Enabler, Encourager, Helper, Teacher, Spirit of truth, Spirit of life, Spirit of glory, Spirit of wisdom and understanding, the names continue. But what is in a name? They were in the dark about what was going to happen that morning.

But why am I telling you this? Were you not there when the Spirit filled the room? Were you there with Peter and Mary and the rest of the 120 when the Spirit came? Isn't that what happens in worship? In the opening of the worship service we pray for the presence of the Spirit. When we ask the illumination of our hearts and minds as we read and preach from Scripture, we entrust our deepest thanksgivings and intercessions to the Spirit. In the benediction we are commissioned in the power of the Spirit. Were you not there? The Corinthians are there:

> A word of wisdom is given by the Spirit to one person, a word of knowledge to another according to the same Spirit, faith to still another by the same Spirit, gifts of healing to another in the one Spirit, performance of miracles to another, prophecy to another, the ability to tell spirits apart to another, different kinds of tongues to another, and the interpretation of the tongues to another. (1 Cor 12:8-10)

The Galatians are there, "But the fruit of the Spirit is love, joy, peace, patience, kindness, goodness, faithfulness, gentleness, and self-control" (Gal 5:22-23).

The original disciples did not sit still on their benches for long when the Holy Spirit came upon them with the sound of an earthquake. They did not just pause, check it out, and go on fiddling with their iPhones. You don't have God's holy flame rest on your neighbor's forehead and talk as though nothing is happening, chatting about socks that disappear in the wash. You don't experience the cleansing fire of God's love in your heart and just sit admiring your manicure. You don't look into the heart and soul of your neighbor, all the suffering and pain, yet all the goodness and joy, and not know you are on holy ground. You don't, because this is a new beginning. You don't experience truth setting up shop, a church being born, neighbors being bonded to neighbors, couples being reconciled, teens finding purpose, prisoners being set free, the lame being healed, and not know you are on holy ground, because this is a new beginning. You don't witness the blind regaining sight, the deaf hearing, the addicts giving up addiction, the rich sharing their wealth, the leaders repenting and not know you are on holy ground, because this is a new beginning. You don't smell "the aroma of Christ" (2 Cor 2:15), even just a whiff, without getting up and saying, Hallelujah! In that moment, "at the name of Jesus everyone / in heaven, on earth, and under the earth might bow / and every tongue confess that / Jesus Christ is Lord, to the glory of God the Father" (Phil 2:10-11).

They had to get up, they had to push those benches to the side, they had to move, they had to get out of doors where even the heavens could not contain their excitement and they couldn't help but witness to their startled neighbors. This was the power of God they had been longing for, that all may be one, Christ present, through the Spirit in their midst.

This was the power of God they had been longing for, that all may be one, Christ present, through the Spirit in their midst.

The truth of Pentecost is not a what but a who, and even then not a *vous* but a *tu.* Pentecost truth is the poetry of an ongoing relationship with Christ through the Spirit, knowing the truth that is God. Jesus said, "I have much more to say to you, but you can't handle it now. However, when the Spirit of Truth comes, he will guide you in all truth" (John 16:12-13), the Advocate, who "won't speak on his own, but will say whatever he hears and will proclaim to you what is to come" (John 16:13). What is to come at the end of time is already received in foretaste in the events of Pentecost: true harmony, union with God, oneness in Christ, life in the Spirit.

In math, a community is the sum of the numbers. In poetry, a community is the sum finding its oneness in Christ. Whenever this happens it is Pentecost again and the new creation is underway. It is not just for the church; it is for its neighbors and all people, "that they all may be one" (John 17:21 KJV). For those on whom the Spirit descends, the power of God's ministry courses through their veins.

Transforming Truth

The New Testament is written in the light provided by Pentecost flames. Scripture is not only inspired by the Spirit. From the first chapter of each Gospel, the writers speak of the Spirit in ways that anticipate the descent of the Spirit on the church that happens in Acts. Mark speaks of the Spirit descending on Jesus "like a dove" (1:10). Luke says the child will be "filled with the Holy Spirit" (1:15), the same words he uses in Acts when the disciples are "filled with the Holy Spirit" (2:4). Twice Matthew says Jesus is "from the Holy Spirit" (1:18, 20 NRSV). Every faithful activity of the church in the Bible presumes the Spirit and that the followers of Jesus "receive power" when the Spirit comes upon them (Acts 1:8). Thus Paul speaks "with a demonstration of the Spirit and of power" (1 Cor 2:4); his words bear truth to his people. He describes the Corinthians "as ministers of a new covenant, not based on what is written but on the Spirit, because what is written kills, but the Spirit gives life" (2 Cor 3:6). The "power" is evident in the gifts of the Spirit that the church receives.

Even ascension, ten days ahead of Pentecost, is recorded in anticipation of Pentecost yet these two events of Jesus pose a conundrum in math. On one hand, he "was lifted up into heaven and sat down on the right side of God" (Mark 16:19). On the other, Jesus says, "I myself will be with you every day until the end of this present age" (Matt 28:20). In math it is not possible to be in two places at once, but in the poetry of God, both claims are valid and the Holy Spirit is the means. Poetry is God's frequent code for "I still have many things to say to you, but you cannot bear them now" (John 16:12 NRSV).

The giving of the Spirit of truth is the gift of a renewing, transformative power. With the Spirit present, churches do not have to rely on being all the same, and can say with the Ephesians, "speaking the truth with love, let's grow in every way into Christ" (Eph 4:15). The Spirit transforms the disciples into a church, one body in service to the world. Baptism, communion, prayer, preaching, worship, outreach, beauty, goodness, truth—all are evidence of this transforming power. Yet this power is not that of brute force, armies, or war, for as Isaiah says of the Servant, "a bruised reed he will not break, / and a dimly burning wick he will not quench; / he will faithfully bring forth justice" (Isa 42:3 NRSV). Paul seems to speak of the same tenderness: "God's kingdom isn't about words but about power. Which do you want? Should I come to you with a big stick to punish you, or with love and a gentle spirit?" (1 Cor 4: 20-21).

Several years ago a bishop in Florida was approached by a woman in his congregation. "I want to make some blankets for the five men who sleep outside the church," she said. The bishop responded, "Is this something that would be easy for you to do?" "Oh yes," she said. The bishop replied, "I was just wondering because I think that when God calls us to do something, it is something that stretches us, and we receive from it. Why don't you make blankets for all the homeless people in the city?" Maybe that was the bishop's version of 1 + 1 = 3. The woman was challenged by his comment, organized several people, and together they made over two thousand blankets. That is the transformative power of the Spirit at work. That is what the sermon should lead to: joy and excitement, thanksgiving and praise, vision and empowerment for ministry. The story is in us and we are in the story. The poetry is in us, and Christ is the poem.

The Ending Says It All

That is why the ending of the sermon needs to overflow with hope, speaking the truth in love—many African American churches call it celebration. People come into church often worn down with the cares of the world. Even if they do not, the first part of the sermon serves to make them attentive to the truth of the suffering around them, and awakens them soberly to the sin and brokenness in their midst. The preacher works hard with the help of the Spirit to bring hope to tough troublous situations, to name what the good news might be, the God news. Every week the Spirit performs the miracle of the sermon, changing the water of life's circumstances into the rich wine of God's comfort, empowerment, and hope. Preachers may speak of deeds that need to be done, but even their language at the end of the sermon shows evidence of the resurrection and the inbreaking of the new creation: *musts, should,* and *have tos* are transformed to life-giving phrases like, *you may now, nothing can prevent you from, you are empowered in this moment to*...

What it all comes down to is this: Preachers have a treasure to give to the world, a pearl of great price (Matt 13:44-46). Preachers need to be joyous in giving it, not down at the mouth. Australian preacher David Cook "likens preaching to an airplane journey. Most energy and concentration are required at the beginning and the end. The takeoff and landing are the most dangerous and require the greatest engine thrust. In between, while airborne, the plane may cruise along. In preaching, beginnings and endings matter the most. 'Maximum thrust at the beginning; maximum thrust at the end.'"[1]

Preaching is theopoetry. It offers God's beauty, goodness, and truth to the world and thereby offers meaning to life. In these pages we could have used values other than beauty, goodness, and truth to explore God's word, but these are chosen for this moment in time when the church needs new ways of walking in the world and new ways to converse with the culture around us. Here we have revisioned preaching as theopoetry, in deliberate contrast to the math that the world so often uses for data, quick answers, new links, the next happening. Theopoetry is also in contrast to the Enlightenment overemphasis on reason, logic, and epistemological foundations. Beauty, goodness, and truth in their fixed modernist expressions are undermined. Language has changed how we think about things. However, beauty, goodness, and truth, reconceived in new ways that are fluid, relational, and poetic, are what the church offers the postmodern world. Sooner or later the postmodern age will pass, and it will be replaced by the next set of influences and trends. Many changes will remain. Language will never be the same as it once was. For now, at least, theopoetry offers not only a way forward but also a better way that expects to find God around each new corner. Christ is the poem, and our lives are Christ's poetry.

Notes

Introduction

1. Eugene H. Peterson, *Tell It Slant: A Conversation on the Language of Jesus in His Stories and Prayers* (Grand Rapids and Cambridge, UK: William B. Eerdmans Publishing Company, 2008).

2. Kevin J. Vanhoozer, *Remythologizing Theology: Divine Action, Passion, and Authorship*. Cambridge Studies in Christian Doctrine (Cambridge and New York: Cambridge University Press, 2010).

One: Preaching as Poetry in an Age of Math (Theory)

1. Cited by Edward Frenkel, "Is the Universe a Simulation?" *New York Times Sunday Review* (February 14, 2014), accessed on February 16, 2014, http://www.nytimes.com/2014/02/16/opinion/sunday/is-the-universe-a-simulation.html?hp&rref=opinion&_r=0Math. He is citing from Kurt Gödel, *Collected Works*, vol. III (Oxford: Clarendon Press and New York: Oxford University Press, 1995, p. 320).

2. This is not true of theoretical math, for instance of Kurt Gödel in his series of incompleteness theorems. Following him, the rationalist system that postmodernism critiques is not a closed system in that it always involves something that is not accountable in the system itself. See Francesco Berto, *There's Something about Gödel: The Complete Guide to the Incompleteness Theorem* (Chichester, UK: Blackwell Publishing Ltd., 2009), esp. 47–51. See also his section on mathematics as faith, 162–70.

3. Thomas H. Troeger, *Wonder Reborn: Creating Sermons on Hymns, Music, and Poetry* (New York: Oxford University Press, 2010).

4. Aristotle, *The Complete Works of Aristotle*, The Revised Oxford Translation, 2 vols., Jonathan Barnes, ed. (Princeton, N.J.: Princeton University Press, 1991), 1:246.

5. Ibid., 1:389.

6. Ibid., 2:1600.

7. Horace Bushnell, "Our Gospel, a Gift to the Imagination" in Conrad Cherry, ed., *Horace Bushnell: Sermons* (New York: Paulist Press, 1985), 100.

8. H. Grady Davis, *Design for Preaching* (Philadelphia: Fortress Press, 1958), 15.

9. David James Randolph, *The Renewal of Preaching* (Philadelphia: Fortress Press: 1969), 22–23.

10. Fred Craddock, *As One Without Authority* (Enid, Okla.: Phillips University Press, 1971).

11. M. Craig Barnes, *The Pastor as Minor Poet: Texts and Subtexts in the Ministerial Life* (Grand Rapids: William B. Eerdmans Publishing Company, 2009), 19.

12. Gaston Bachelard, *The Poetics of Space*, trans. John R. Stigloe (Boston: Beacon Press, 1969), xx. Cited in James K. A. Smith, *Imagining the Kingdom: How Worship Works* (Grand Rapids: Baker Academic, 2013), 18n39.

13. Smith, 19.

14. Amos N. Wilder, *Theopoetic: Theology and the Religious Imagination* (Philadelphia: Fortress Press, 1976), 5.

15. Ibid., 2.

16. Ibid., 13.

17. Stanley Romaine Hopper, cited from an interview with Dan Noel at Drew University in 1977, in David Miller, "Stanley Hopper and Mythopoetics," *ARC*, an online journal of The Society for the Arts, Religion, and Contemporary Culture, accessed on April 24, 2013, http://www.sarcc.org/Hopper.htm.

18. Stanley R. Hopper, "The Literary Imagination and the Doing of Theology," in R. Melvin Keiser and Tony Stoneburner, eds., *The Way of Transfiguration: Religious Imagination as Theopoiesis* (Louisville: Westminster/John Knox, 1992), 224.

19. Wilder, 1.

20. L. B. C. Keefe-Perry, "Divine Exploration and Invitation," in *CrossCurrents*, Issue 1 (March 2010): 98.

21. Callid Keefe-Perry, website, "Religion and Spirituality," accessed on April 20, 2013, http://callidkeefeperry.com/religion-and-spirituality. Keefe-Perry maintains what is claimed to be the largest online hub of information on theopoetics at THEOPOETICS(dot)NET.

22. Smith, 33–34.

23. Ibid., 32.

24. Ibid.

25. Ibid., 32n2.

26. Scott Holland, "Theology Is a Kind of Writing: The Emergence of Theopoetics," *CrossCurrents* 47, no. 3 (1997): 327.

27. L. B. C. Keefe-Perry, "Theopoetics: Process and Perspective," *Christianity and Literature* 58, no. 4 (2009): 581.

Two: The Beauty of Faith (Homiletics)

1. Wladyslaw Tatarkiewicz, "The Great Theory of Beauty and Its Decline," *Journal of Aesthetics and Art Criticism* XXXI (Winter 1972): 165–80.

2. Duns Scotus Erigena as cited by Edward Farley, *Faith and Beauty: A Theological Aesthetic* (Burlington, Ver.: Ashgate Publishing Limited, 2001), 21.

3. Hugh of St. Victor, *The Didascalion of Hugh of St. Victor: A Medieval Guide to the Arts*, trans. Jerome Taylor (New York and London: Columbia University Press, 1961), 2:4, 64.

4. G. R. Evans, *The Language and Logic of the Bible: The Earlier Middle Ages* (Cambridge, UK: Cambridge University Press, 1984), 1. See also Paul Scott Wilson, *God Sense: Reading the Bible for Preaching* (Nashville: Abingdon Press, 2001), which explores the relevance of the four senses for today.

5. Jean-François Lyotard, *The Postmodern Condition: A Report on Knowledge*, Theory and History of Literature, vol. 10, trans. Geoff Bennington and Brian Massumi (Minneapolis: University of Minneapolis, 1984 [original French version, 1979]), 77.

6. *The Random House Dictionary of the English Language* (New York: Random House, 1969).

7. M. Craig Barnes, *Pastor as Minor Poet* (Grand Rapids: William B. Eerdmans, 2009), dedication page.

8. Edward Farley, *Faith and Beauty: A Theological Aesthetic* (Burlington, Vt.: Ashgate Publishing Limited, 2001), 101–3.

9. Gerard Manley Hopkins, "God's Grandeur," *The Poems of Gerard Manley Hopkins*, 4th ed. (Oxford: Oxford University Press, 1970), 66.

10. Simone Weil, *Waiting on God*, trans. Emma Craufurd (New York: Harper Perennial Modern Classics, 2009), 112, 101. Cited by Patrick Sherry, *Spirit and Beauty* (London, SCM Press, 2002), 69.

11. Space and Science Writer for *Time Magazine*, Michael Lemonick, in an interview with Judy Woodruff on *PBS Newshour* (August 16, 2013), accessed on September 16, 2013, http://www.pbs.org/newshour/bb/science/july-dec13/kepler_08-16.html.

12. Jeremy S. Begbie, "Created Beauty: The Witness of J. S. Bach," in Daniel J. Treier, Mark Husbands, and Roger Lundin, *The Beauty of God: Theology and the Arts*, Downers Grove, Illinois: InterVarsity Press, 2006), 25.

13. Augustine, *Confessions* (Oxford, UK: Oxford University Press, 1999), 201 (X:xxvii [38]). I am grateful in this paragraph for a conversation with Sam Persons Parkes.

14. I have written at length on the nature of the gospel in *The Practice of Preaching*, rev. ed. (Nashville: Abingdon Press, 2007), and *Setting Words on Fire: Putting God at the Center of the Sermon* (Nashville: Abingdon Press, 2008).

15. Howard Gardner, *Truth, Beauty, and Goodness Reframed: Educating for the Virtues in the Twenty-First Century* (New York: Basic Books, 2011), 48.

16. Begbie, "Created Beauty," 29.

17. William Carl Placher, *The Domestication of Transcendence: How Modern Thinking about God Went Wrong* (Louisville: Westminster John Knox Press, 1996), 7.

18. Ibid., 6.

19. Howard Gardner, *Truth, Beauty, and Goodness Reframed: Educating for the Virtues in the Twenty-First Century* (New York: Basic Books, 2011), 50.

20. Paul Scott Wilson, *The Four Pages of the Sermon* (Nashville: Abingdon Press, 1999), 33–57.

21. Anita Patil, "The Crowds That Shun the Mass Market," in *New York Times*, insert in the *Toronto Star* (Sunday, June 10, 2012): 1.

22. Bill Pennington, "Looking for Lower Scores? Use Your Eyes and Ears," *New York Times* (August 17, 2008), accessed on March 20, 2012, http://www.nytimes.com/2008/08/18/sports/golf/18pennington.html?pagewanted=all.

23. Paul Scott Wilson, ed., *Abingdon Theological Companion to the Lectionary, Preaching Years A, B, and C* (Nashville: Abingdon Press, 2011–2014).

24. He calls these qualities "symptoms antecedent to the experience of beauty." Gardner, *Truth*, 50.

25. Ibid., 49. See 49–54.

26. Ibid., 51.

27. Ibid., 53–55.

Three: Christmas Strategies for Beauty (Practice)

1. Stephen Crites, "The Narrative Quality of Experience," *Journal of the American Academy of Religion* 39, no. 3 (September 1, 1971): 291–311.

2. Video clip in Maria Popova, "1 + 1 = 3: Ken Burns on What Makes a Great Story," *Brain Pickings*, accessed on July 23, 2012, http://www.brainpickings.org/index.php/2012/05/17/ken-burns-on-stories/

3. Ibid.

4. See Aristotle, *The Complete Works of Aristotle, The Revised Oxford Translation*, ed. Jonathan Barnes (Princeton, N.J.: Princeton University Press, 1991), 2:2324.

5. Eric Auerbach, *Mimesis: The Representation of Reality in Western Literature*, Princeton Classics Edition, trans. Willard R. Trask (Princeton, N.J.: Princeton University Press, 2013 [1953]), 8–22.

6. Horace Bushnell, *Christ and His Salvation* (London: Richard D. Dickenson, 1880), 4–6.

7. Martin Buber, *Tales of the Hasidim: The Early Masters* (New York: Schocken Books, Inc., 1947), v–vi.

Four: Is Good Just Relative Now? (Theory)

1. Clark M. Williamson, "Proper 8 [13]," *Abingdon Theological Companion to the Lectionary, Preaching Year B* (Nashville: Abingdon Press, 2014), 203.

2. Gene Weingarten, "Pearls before Breakfast: Can One of the Nation's Great Musicians Cut through the Fog of a D.C. Rush Hour?" *Washington Post* (Sunday, April 8, 2007), accessed on March 20, 2009, http://www.washingtonpost.com/wp-dyn/content/article/2007/04/04/AR2007040401721.html

3. Stanley G. Clarke and Evan Simpson, "Introduction: The Primacy of Moral

Practice," in *Anti-Theory in Ethics and Moral Conservatism*, eds. Stanley G. Clark and Evan Simpson (Albany: State University of New York Press, 1989), 1.

4. "Hermeneutics seems to me to be animated by this double motivation: willingness to suspect, willingness to listen; vow of rigor, vow of obedience." Paul Ricoeur, *Freud and Philosophy: An Essay on Interpretation* (New Haven: Yale University Press, 1970), 27.

5. Howard Gardner, *Truth, Beauty, and Goodness Reframed: Educating for the Virtues in the Twenty-First Century* (New York: Basic Books, 2011), 98.

6. Ibid., 98.

7. David Brooks, "The Moral Diet," in *New York Times* (June 7, 2012), accessed on June 7, 2013, http://www.nytimes.com/2012/06/08/opinion/brooks-the-moral-diet.html?_r=1&ref=global-home.

8. Ferdinand de Saussure, *Course in General Linguistics*, eds. Perry Meisel and Haun Saussy, trans. Wade Baskin (New York: Columbia University Press, 2011).

9. Jacques Derrida, *Of Grammatology*, trans. Gayatri Chakravorty Spivak (Baltimore and London: The John Hopkins University Press, 1976 [French, 1967]), 65.

10. Ibid., 65.

11. Ibid., 71.

12. Jack Reynolds, "Jacques Derrida (1930–2004)," *Internet Encyclopedia of Philosophy: A Peer-Reviewed Academic Resource*, Section 6b, accessed on June 11, 2013, http://www.iep.utm.edu/derrida/. He cites Derrida in "Psyche: Inventions of the Other" in *Reading De Man Reading*, eds. Waters and Godzich (Minneapolis: University of Minnesota Press, 1989), 60.

13. Jacques Derrida, "Derrida on Prayer, Part 2," Interview at a conference entitled *Derrida and Religion: Other Testaments*, University of Toronto, Toronto (November 23–26, 2002), accessed on June 13, 2013, http://www.youtube.com/watch?v=MG_nyd45czM.

14. Ibid.

15. Jacques Derrida, "Différance," *Margins of Philosophy*, trans. Alan Bass (Chicago and London: Chicago University Press, 1982), 5–45.

16. For the importance of preaching as teaching, testimony, and proclamation, see Paul Scott Wilson, *Setting Words on Fire: Putting God at the Center of the Sermon* (Nashville: Abingdon Press, 2008).

17. "The activity or productivity connoted by the idea of différance refers to the generative movement in the play of differences. The latter are neither fallen from the sky nor inscribed once and for all in a closed system, a static structure that a synchronic and taxonomic operation could exhaust. Differences are the effects of transformations, and from this vantage the theme of différance is incompatible with the static, synchronic, taxonomic, ahistoric motifs in the concept of structure." Jacques Derrida, "Interview with Julia Kristeva" in *Positions*, trans. Alan Bass (Chicago: University of Chicago Press, 1981), 29. See also Derrida, *Grammatology*, 23, 63.

18. See George Lindbeck, *The Nature of Doctrine* (Louisville: Westminster John Knox Press, 1984).

19. See Jacques Derrida, *Acts of Religion* (New York: Routledge, 2002), 243.

20. Shyh-Jen Fuh, "Derrida and the Problem of Ethics," *Concentric: Studies in English Literature and Linguistics* 29, no. 1 (January 2003): 1.

21. Ibid., 19.

22. Ibid., 20.

23. Troy Jollimore, "Godless but Good," *Aeon Magazine*, a digital magazine published February 18, 2013, accessed on February 18, 2013, http://www.aeonmagazine.com/world-views/troy-jollimore-secular-ethics/.

24. John McClure, *Other-wise Preaching* (St. Louis: Chalice Press, 2001), ix.

25. Graham Ward, "Introduction to Walter Lowe," in Graham Ward, ed., *Blackwell Companion to Postmodern Theology* (Malden, Mass.: Blackwell Publishers, 2001), 491.

26. Phil Snider, *Preaching after God: Derrida, Caputo, and the Language of Postmodern Homiletics* (Eugene, Ore.: Cascade Books, 2012).

Five: Acts of Goodness (Homiletics)

1. Frederick Beuchner, *Telling the Truth: The Gospel as Tragedy, Comedy, and Fairy Tale* (San Francisco: Harper and Row, 1977), 7.

2. M. Craig Barnes, *The Pastor as Minor Poet: Texts and Subtexts in the Ministerial Life* (Grand Rapids, Michigan: William B. Eerdmans Publishing Company, 2009), 125.

3. Hans Urs von Balthasar, *Truth Is Symphonic: Aspects of Christian Pluralism* (San Francisco: Ignatius Press, 1987), 13.

4. Derrida, "Derrida on Prayer, Part 2," interview at a conference entitled *Derrida and Religion: Other Testaments*, University of Toronto, Toronto, November 23-26, 2002. Viewed online on 06/13/2013 at http://www.youtube.com/watch?v=MG_nyd45czM. Theologian Serene Jones says something similar. She points to law and gospel as "double signs" of the church that allow for the kind of community that secular feminist theorists long for, communities of "bounded openness . . . in which boundaries exist for the sake of establishing a ruled community whose very identity rests in its openness. . . . Marked by Gospel, the church stands as a community freed to be for the world to be witnesses to a grace that embraces all. Marked by Law, it is also a community who in its freedom seeks to witness to the Gospel by embodying practices, disciplines, and rules that give to this grace material form." Serene Jones, "Companionable Wisdoms: What Insights Might Feminist Theorists Gather from Feminist Theologians?" in *The Blackwell Companion to Postmodern Theology*, ed. Graham Ward (Oxford, UK, and Malden, Mass.: Blackwell Publishers, 2001), 302.

5. Joanna Adams, quoted in *Best Advice for Preaching*, ed. John S. McClure (Minneapolis: Fortress Press, 1998), 7.

6. Cleophus J. LaRue, *The Heart of Black Preaching* (Louisville: Westminster John Knox Press, 2000), 69.

7. Eugene H. Peterson, *Tell It Slant: A Conversation on the Language of Jesus in His Stories and Prayers* (Grand Rapids and Cambridge, UK: William B. Eerdmans Publishing Company, 2008), 11.

8. I have responded to one critic on this matter in Paul Scott Wilson, *The Practice of Preaching*, rev. ed. (Nashville: Abingdon Press, 2007), 179–83. For a review of the history of law and gospel, see Paul Scott Wilson, *Preaching and Homiletical Theory* (St. Louis: Chalice Press, 2004), 73–86.

9. The following two tables are from my *Practice of Preaching* (Nashville: Abingdon Press, 2007), 245. Used by permission.

10. See Paul Scott Wilson, *The Four Pages of the Sermon: A Guide to Biblical Preaching* (Nashville: Abingdon Press, 1996).

11. The full text of this sermon may be found in Paul Scott Wilson, "A Goat's Perspective: Matthew 25:31-46," *Ex Auditu* 20 (2004): 162–65.

12. Claude Lévi-Strauss, *The Savage Mind* (Chicago: University of Chicago Press, 1966 [Fr. 1962]), 16.

13. Luke A. Powery, *Dem Dry Bones: Preaching, Death, and Hope* (Minneapolis: Fortress Press, 2013).

14. The rhizome was conceived as an alternate model for thought in opposition to the modern vertical model of a tree whose roots can be traced to their origin and that aims toward some high achievement. Gilles Deleuze and Félix Guttari, *A Thousand Plateaus: Capitalism and Schizophrenia* (Minneapolis: University of Minnesota, 1987), 23–28.

15. Nancy Duarte, "The Secret of Great Talks," TED: Ideas Worth Spreading, Filmed Nov. 2011, Posted Feb. 2012, TEDxEast, accessed on March 15, 2013, http://www.ted.com/talks/nancy_duarte_the_secret_structure_of_great_talks.html.

16. Barnes, 131.

17. Angélique Du Toit, "Postmodernism and Organizations," in Stuart Sim, ed., *The Routledge Companion to Postmodernism*, 3rd ed. (London and New York: Routledge, 2011), 113.

18. Ibid., 112.

19. Wendy J. Austin, "Relational Ethics," *The SAGE Encyclopedia of Qualitative Research Methods*, ed. Lisa M. Given, Thousand Oaks, Cal: SAGE Publications, Inc., 2008. 749-50. SAGE knowledge. Web http://knowledge.sagepub.com/view/research/n378.xml. 19 Sept. 2013.

20. Ibid.

21. Ron Allen, "Proper 5 [10]," *Abingdon Theological Companion to the Lectionary*, Year B (Nashville: Abingdon Press, 2014), 187.

22. Michel Foucault, "On the Genealogy of Ethics: An Overview of Work in Progress," an interview conducted by Paul Rabinow and Hubert Dreyfus in April 1983, in Michel Foucault, *Ethics: Subjectivity and Truth*, ed. Paul Rabinow, trans. Robert Hurley (New York: New Press, 1997), 298.

23. Jean Baudrillard, *The Transparency of Evil: Essays on Extreme Phenomena*, trans. James Benedict (London and New York: Verso, 1993), 92.

24. Ibid., 93.

25. Ibid., 92.

26. Ibid., 94.

27. Martha Stortz, "Second Sunday in Advent," *Abingdon Theological Companion to the Lectionary*, Year A (Nashville: Abingdon Press, 2013), 23.

Six: What Easter Deconstructs (Practice)

1. Ron Allen, "Proper 5 [10]," *Abingdon Theological Companion to the Lectionary*, Year B (Nashville: Abingdon Press, 2014), 199.

2. John Donne, "Good Friday, 1613. Riding Westward," Poems (London: M. F. for John Marriot, 1633), accessed on January 21, 2014, http://homes.chass.utoronto.ca/~ian/donne34.html.

3. Paul Scott Wilson, "Fifth Sunday after the Epiphany [5]," in Paul Scott Wilson, ed., *Abingdon Theological Companion to the Lectionary*, Year B (Nashville: Abingdon Press, 2014), 74.

4. George Herbert, "Easter Wings," *The Temple* (1633), accessed on January 21, 2014, http://www.ccel.org/h/herbert/temple/Easterwings.html.

5. Kevin J. Vanhoozer, *The Drama of Doctrine: A Canonical-Linguistic Approach to Christian Theology* (Louisville: Westminster John Knox Press, 2005), 59.

6. Ibid., 102.

7. Ibid., 180.

8. Ibid., 254.

9. Samuel Wells, *Improvisation: The Drama of Christian Ethics* (Grand Rapids: Brazos Press, 2004), 131–34.

10. Ibid., 143–53. Vanhoozer has his own version of reincorporating, see: *The Drama of Doctrine*, 339–40.

11. Wells, 151.

12. Ibid., 124.

13. Sally Brown, "5th Sunday in Lent," *The Abingdon Theological Companion to the Lectionary*, Year B (Nashville: Abingdon Press, 2014), 115.

14. Heather Stevenson preached this in a class sermon at Emmanuel College, March 5, 2013.

15. These refrains are adapted from my *Setting Words on Fire: Putting God at the Center of the Sermon* (Nashville: Abingdon Press, 2008), 149–210. They are examples of proclamation as opposed to teaching, even though they also teach.

16. Martin Luther, "Lectures on Galatians 1519," cited in Charles B. Cousar, *Galatians*, Interpretation, A Bible Commentary for Teaching and Preaching (Louisville: John Knox Press, 1982), 145.

17. Richard Rohr, "Richard Rohr's Daily Meditation," [no date], accessed on September 26, 2013, web: http://myemail.constantcontact.com/Richard-Rohr-s-Meditation—Will-Anyone-Second-the-Motion-.html?soid=1103098668616&aid=_KmgN31c7ig.

18. Kenneth A. Myers, *All God's Children and Blue Suede Shoes* (Westchester, Ill.: Crossways Books, 1989), 85.

19. Jeremy S. Begbie, "Beauty, Sentimentality and the Arts," in Daniel J. Treier, Mark Husbands, and Roger Lundin, *The Beauty of God: Theology and the Arts* (Downers Grove, Ill.: InterVarsity Press, 2006), 61.

20. Ibid., 47.
21. Ibid., 51.
22. Ibid., 52.
23. Ibid., 66.

Seven: Truth as Event (Theory)

1. Stanley J. Grenz, *A Primer on Postmodernism* (Grand Rapids: William B. Eerdmans Publishing Company, 1996), 38.

2. Jacques Derrida, *Of Grammatology*, trans. Gayatri Chakravorty Spivak (Baltimore and London: The John Hopkins University Press, 1976 [French, 1967]), 158.

3. See Howard Gardner, *Frames of the Mind: The Theory of Multiple Intelligences* (New York: Basic Books, 2011 [1983]).

4. David J. Lose, *Preaching at the Crossroads: How the World—and Our Preaching—Is Changing* (Minneapolis: Fortress Press, 2013), 32.

5. Even the medieval phrase for sworn testimony recognizes different ways truth may be practiced, namely, "the truth (= what the witness actually experienced), the whole truth (= nothing omitted), and nothing but the truth (= no lies)."

6. American Dialect Society official website, accessed on December 8, 2013, http://www.americandialect.org/truthiness_voted_2005_word_of_the_year.

7. Angélique Du Toit, "Postmodernism and Organizations," in Stuart Sim, ed., *The Routledge Companion to Postmodernism*, 3rd ed. (London and New York: Routledge, 2011), 110.

8. See Mark Slouka, *War of the Worlds: Cyberspace and the High-Tech Assault on Reality* (New York: Basic Books, 1995).

9. Kevin Vanhoozer, "Scripture and Tradition," in Kevin Vanhoozer, ed., *The Cambridge Companion to Postmodern Theology* (Cambridge, U.K. and New York: Cambridge University Press, 2003), 157.

10. Margaret Avison, "First," *The Dumbfounding: Poems* (New York: Norton Publishers, 1966), 51.

11. Emily Dickinson, *The Complete Poems*, ed. Thomas H. Johnson (Boston: Little, Brown and Company, 1955), 506.

12. "New Year Letter," *Collected Longer Poems of W. H. Auden* (New York: Random House, 1965), 79.

13. Eugene H. Peterson, *Tell It Slant: A Conversation on the Language of Jesus in His Stories and Prayers* (Grand Rapids and Cambridge, UK: William B. Eerdmans Publishing Company, 2008), 4.

14. Serge F. Kovaleski, "Killers' Families Left to Confront Fear and Shame," *New York Times* (February 5, 2012), accessed May 2, 2013, http://www.nytimes.com/2012/02/05/us/killers-families-left-to-confront-fear-and-shame.html?hp.

15. Cahill, cited in "Killers' Families."

16. David Bentley Hart, *The Beauty of the Infinite: The Aesthetics of Christian Truth* (Grand Rapids: Wm. B. Eerdmans Publishing Co., 2003), 3.

17. Jean-François Lyotard, *The Postmodern Condition: A Report on Knowledge*,

Theory and History of Literature, 10, trans. Geoff Bennington and Brian Massumi (Minneapolis: The University of Minnesota Press, 1984), xxiv.

18. Ibid., xxiii–xiv.

19. Others find decline in the Enlightenment narrative in the decay of the "progress myth" beginning with World War I and the Great Depression. Richard J. Middleton and Brian Walsh. *Truth Is Stranger Than It Used to Be: Biblical Faith in a Postmodern Age* (Downers Grove: InterVarsity Press, 1995), 20–23.

20. Lyotard, 81.

21. Ibid., 15.

22. Ibid.

23. Lowe says postmodernism is "against any policing or narrowing of public discourse in the name of one singularity or another." Walter Lowe, "Is There a Postmodern Gospel?" in Graham Ward, ed., *Blackwell Companion to Postmodern Theory*, (Malden, Mass.: Blackwell Publishers, 2001), 496.

24. Stuart Sim, "Preface to the Third Edition," in Stuart Sim, ed., *The Routledge Companion to Postmodernism*, 3rd ed. (London and New York: Routledge, 2011), vii.

25. Ibid., vii–viii.

26. Jean-François Lyotard, *The Differend: Phrases in Dispute*, trans. Georges Van Den Abbeele. (Manchester: Manchester University Press, 1988), 135.

27. I. A. Richards, *Science and Poetry* (New York: W. W. Norton and Company, 1926), 34–35.

28. Kevin J. Vanhoozer, *The Drama of Doctrine: a Canonical-Linguistic Approach to Christian Theology* (Louisville: Westminster John Knox Press, 2005), 62.

29. Hart, 3.

30. Paul Ricoeur, *Figuring the Sacred: Religion, Narrative, and Imagination*, ed. Mark I. Wallace, trans. David Pellauer (Minneapolis: Fortress Press, 1995), 144.

31. Hayden White, *Tropics of Discourse* (Baltimore: Johns Hopkins University Press, 1978), 121. See also p. 98.

32. Daniel Aaron, "What Can You Learn from a Historical Novel?" *American Heritage* 43, no. 6 (1992): 1, accessed September 9, 2013 at http://www.americanheritage.com/content/what-can-you-learn-historical-novel1992.

33. Ibid., 1.

34. Zhang Longxi, *Allegoresis: Reading Canonical Literature East and West* (London and New York: Cornell University Press, 2005), 46.

35. Ibid., 57–58.

36. Ibid., 46.

37. I first explored these ideas in my *Imagination of the Heart: New Understandings in Preaching* (Nashville: Abingdon Press, 1988). For a more in-depth treatment of Coleridge's ideas on imagination see my article, "*Biographia*'s Coherence: God, Self, and Coleridge's 'Seminal Principle,'" in *Philological Quarterly* 72, no. 4 (Fall, 1993): 451–69.

38. See Luke A. Powery, *Spirit Speech: Lament and Celebration in Preaching* (Nashville: Abingdon Press, 2009).

39. James M. Childs, "Doctrines and Biblical Texts," in Paul Scott Wilson, gen. ed., *The New Interpreter's Handbook of Preaching* (Nashville: Abingdon Press, 2008), 450.

40. Henry Blackeby, *Spiritual Leadership: Moving People on to God's Agenda* (Nashville: B&H Publishing, 2011).

41. David Brooks, "The Art of Presence," *New York Times* (January 20, 2014), accessed on January 21, 2014, http://www.nytimes.com/2014/01/21/opinion/brooks-the-art-of-presence.html?action=click&contentCollection=Automobiles&module=MostEmailed&version=Full&region=Marginalia&src=me&pgtype=article.

Eight: Truth and Worship (Homiletics)

1. David J. Lose, *Preaching at the Crossroads: How the World—and Our Preaching—Is Changing* (Minneapolis: Fortress Press, 2013), 75–76.

2. Don Tapscott, "A New Reason to Support the CBC," Toronto Star (July 31, 2011): A11.

3. Sharon Crowley, *Toward a Civil Discourse: Rhetoric and Fundamentalism* (Pittsburgh: University of Pittsburgh Press, 2006), 2–4.

4. Nolan McCarty, Keith T. Poole, and Howard Rosenthal, *Polarized America: The Dance of Ideology and Unequal Riches* (Cambridge, Mass.: Massachusetts Institute of Technology), 2006.

5. Summarized by Mike Brunker, "Wealth in America: White-Minorities Gap Is Now a Chasm," msnbc.com, 07/26/2011, accessed on August 6, 2011, http://www.msnbc.msn.com/id/43887485/from/RSS/#.TjxgPL9WJe4.

6. Thomas Bender, "The Thinning of American Political Culture," in Judith Rodin and Stephen P. Steinberg, *Political Discourse in America: Conversation and Community in the Twenty-First Century* (Pittsburgh: University of Pittsburgh Press, 2003), 27–34.

7. Kenneth J. Gergen, *Social Construction in Context* (London: Sage, 2001), 71–75.

8. Martin Marty, *By Way of Response* (Nashville: Abingdon Press, 1981), 81.

9. Richard J. Mouw, *Uncommon Decency: Christian Civility in an Uncivil World* (Downers Grove, Ill.: InterVarsity Press, 1992), 11.

10. Ibid., 12.

11. Ibid., 13

12. John S. McClure, *The Roundtable Pulpit: Where Leadership and Preaching Meet* (Nashville: Abingdon Press, 1995), 12.

13. Ibid., 48–72.

14. Ibid., 13.

15. Lucy Atkinson Rose, *Sharing the Word, Preaching in the Roundtable Church* (Louisville: Westminster, 1997).

16. See Brian K. Blount, "The Apocalypse of Worship: A House of Prayer for All Nations," in *Making Room at the Table: An Invitation to Multicultural Worship*, ed. Brian K. Blount and Lenora Tubbs Tisdale (Louisville: Westminster John Knox, 2001), 16–29.

17. Justo L. González, *For the Healing of the Nations: The Book of Revelation in an Age of Conflict* (New York: Orbis Pub., 1999), 112.

18. Ronald J. Allen, *Preaching the Topical Sermon* (Louisville: Westminster/John Knox, 1992), 95–112.

19. Jenn Supple, Anne Marie Gruber, and Robert Stephen Reid, *Connecting with Your Audience: Making Public Speaking Matter* (Dubuque, Iowa: Kendall Hunt, 2010), 179–81. The model cited here was developed by Robert Reid. I am very grateful in this next paragraph for conversations with him.

20. Wayne Booth, *The Rhetoric of Rhetoric: The Quest for Effective Communication* (Malden, Mass.: Blackwell Publishing, 2004), 161.

21. Sonja K. Foss and Karen A. Foss, *Inviting Transformation: Presentational Speaking for a Changing World*, 3rd ed. (Long Grove, Ill.: Waveland Press, 2011).

22. O. Wesley Allen, *The Homiletic of All Believers: A Conversational Approach* (Louisville: Westminster John Knox Press, 2005), 17–18.

23. Other conclusions were: (1) leaders in public discourse need to be attracted and trained, (2) public discourse increasingly must acknowledge race and ethnicity, where people come from and who they are, (3) there is a need to locate the boundaries between public and private. Stephen P. Steinberg, "Epilogue: The Centrality of Public Discourse," in Judith Rodin and Stephen P. Steinberg, *Public Discourse in America: Conversation and Community in the Twenty-First Century* (Philadelphia: University of Pennsylvania Press, 2003), 250–52.

24. McClure, 12.

25. Lenora Tubbs Tisdale, "Navigating the Contemporary Worship Narrows: Channel Markers for Deep Waters," in *Making Room at the Table: An Invitation to Multicultural Worship*, ed. Brian K. Blount and Lenora Tubbs Tisdale (Louisville: Westminster John Knox, 2001), 175–90.

26. Brian K. Blount, "The Apocalypse of Worship."

27. Pablo A. Jiménez, "Missional Preaching," in *The New Interpreter's Handbook of Preaching* (Nashville: Abingdon Press, 2008), 278.

28. Luke A. Powery, "Postcolonial Criticism," in *The New Interpreter's Handbook of Preaching* (Nashville: Abingdon Press, 2008), 161.

29. Howard Gardner, *Frames of the Mind: The Theory of Multiple Intelligences* (New York: Basic Books, 2011 [1983]), vii–viii.

30. Bryan D. Spinks, *Worship Mall: Contemporary Responses to Contemporary Culture* (New York: Church Publishing Incorporated, 2011).

31. Barna Group, "Barna Finds Four Mega-Themes in Recent Research" (December 3, 2007), accessed on September 5, 2013, http://www.barna.org/culture-articles/89-barna-finds-four-mega-themes-in-recent-research.

32. I am not an expert in contemporary worship practices. What I propose here is simply my attempt to think through a coherent alternative to traditional

worship. Some churches no doubt already have similar kinds of practice, though perhaps not packaged in this way.

33. Currently we tend to take children out for the sermon, assuming the reason is the problem in commanding their attention. This model might turn that on its head. Perhaps children are fidgety in the sermon because of how long they have had to be still prior to it. Having children present for the sermon might encourage preachers to speak more directly to them and thus be more plain and concrete in their overall speech, to the benefit of all.

34. See David Murrow, *Why Men Hate Going to Church*, rev. ed. (Nashville: Thomas Nelson, 2011).

35. J. Peter Holmes, used by permission.

Nine: Truth as Pentecost Transformation (Practice)

1. David Cook as paraphrased by Simon Vibert, *Excellence in Preaching: Studying the Craft of Leading Preachers* (Downer's Grove, Ill.: InterVarsity Press, 2011), 81.

CPSIA information can be obtained
at www.ICGtesting.com
Printed in the USA
LVHW041618230421
685369LV00017B/766

9 781426 764042